JOB POWER

The Young People's Job-Finding Guide

JOB POWER

The Young People's Job-Finding Guide

by Bernard Haldane, Jean Haldane & Lowell Martin

illustrated by Loel Barr

ACROPOLIS BOOKS LTD.
Washington, D.C.

Reprinted March 1982

© *Revised Copyright 1980, by Bernard Haldane,*
Jean M. Haldane, Lowell B. Martin

© *Copyright 1976 by Bernard Haldane,*
Jean M. Haldane, Lowell B. Martin

ACROPOLIS BOOKS LTD.
Colortone Building, 2400 17th St., N.W.
Washington, D.C. 20009

Printed in the United States of America by
COLORTONE Press, Creative Graphics, Inc.
Washington, D.C. 20009

Library of Congress Cataloging in Publication Data

Haldane, Bernard.
  The young people's job finding guide.

  Published in 1980 under title: Job power.
  Bibliography: p.
  1. Vocational guidance. 2. Job hunting. I. Haldane,
Jean M. II. Martin, Lowell. III. Title.
HF5381.H1314 1982   650.1'4'088055   82-3934
ISBN 0-87491-608-9   AACR2
ISBN 0-87491-609-7 (pbk.)

Dedicated to
the excellence in each person, its
release and fulfilling expression.

Acknowledgements

Experiences with many thousands of men and women of all ages have enabled this book to be written. Its foundations are in the work and concepts of Bernard Haldane, whose background is given in the appendix. The authors are most appreciative of the work of Kelly Bennett who patiently and carefully typed and re-typed the manuscript.

Foreword

IF YOU NEED A JOB, this book will help you overcome the blocks to your success. Federal and State government reports show that the systems given here cut job finding time in half. All of them have been thoroughly tested, and they work well.

Should you be a young man or woman between the ages of sixteen and twenty, the book will give you new ways to deal with old problems. You will find out how to manufacture all the contacts you need, and how to beat the "no experience" rap. You will learn how to get interviews without turndowns, how to get assurance of a pay increase just a few days after you start working and, most importantly, how to identify and develop your best skills and talents.

These systems given are based on experimental work in high schools and colleges, with dropouts and graduates, as well as counseling experience with tens of thousands of clients in all levels of work and non-work. These range from top executives in the American Management Association's President's group to persons dependent on public welfare support.

The authors have been developing and improving their systems since before 1947, when Bernard Haldane Associates was established. You'll find more about the authors and the history of their pioneering organization in the final pages of this book.

Contents

1 Your Future Is Present 1

Obstacles in traditional job finding systems; look for what's right in yourself; develop a Career Journal; start to identify your strengths; get a handle on skills employers want.

2 Unlock Your Potential 19

Three tasks to help you identify the pattern of skills that bring you Achievements: Chart Your Motivated Skills, Target them, Reality Test to clarify your "ideal" job.

3 Job Power Tool 41

How to develop your Job Power Report; use it to overcome traditional put-downs about "no experience;" use it to be many places at once and to answer ads; use it to avoid filling out most job application forms; many examples of Reports.

Introduction

by Bernard Haldane, Ph.D.

FOR THE PAST FOUR DECADES I've studied what people do to get good jobs in bad times and in good ones. I've learned why employers create jobs around the skills and talents of certain people. I've worked out how teachers can get students to learn more, have better classroom discipline, prevent dropouts. I originated ways to help homemakers recognize the valuable skills they acquired in all parts of their lives. For Asian refugees, I researched and worked out how they can learn English faster, get jobs quicker, and bridge more easily into the U.S. culture. With humanities Ph.D.'s, those having the hardest time finding appropriate jobs, I researched and created systems to greatly increase their employability without the need for some special training. My concern for people hit by "burnout" prompted me to develop ways you can use to manage career stress in every part of your life. I've already worked with two generations in families concerned with finding their own paths to fulfilling lives.

This book provides the keys to achieving all these things. It is obviously written for the needs of young adults, yet it includes the principles adults can use to identify their motivated skills — the dependable ones that both turn you on and assure employers of good performance. It gives instructions on how you can get good interviews without turndowns and change yourself from job hunter into job magnet — a person who attracts job offers.

It also tells you how to build a team of supporters who can be of help during the job search, and how to hold on to a job and get ahead in it. At the same time the many systems given here enable you to change jobs or careers with minimum stress.

Let me give an example, using the case history of an Asian refugee, "Jon." He could speak no English, and had been told that in his adopted country he would have to begin all over again; so he must forget what he had learned in his native Vietnam. In one hour, speaking with him through an interpreter, I learned that he had mechanical skills that were first demonstrated at age six when he secretly repaired his mother's sewing machine while she was out shopping. He was punished, of course, because he might have hurt himself. Later he fixed bicycles, motorbikes and cars — all for fun. But when it came to lumber mill equipment repair and maintenance, he was expert. Jon's sponsor, who was present through the interview, had previously known nothing of these experiences; but he was especially interested because he was an executive of a big lumber company. Three weeks later Jon quit the posthole digging job he had taken to earn a few bucks and started work on machine maintenance at $7.50 an hour.

Jon was helped to see himself in terms of how he could be of maximum value to an employer.

Another example, this one involving a grandparent and his grandson Joe, a child of nine in a slum area near Chicago. The child and his sister ran in waving dollar bills. Grandfather was alarmed, wondering where they could have got those bills. But he had worked through Job Power himself and thought he'd try its ideas out with the kids. Instead of gruffly saying, "Where did you get that money?" he said, "What did you do to get that money?" So the kids weren't fearful when they told their story in a breathless rush of words. "We didn't have anything to do so Joe said we could try and build a house in the playground. We found some cardboard, and got some other kids to help us build it. Then Joe said we should have some cookies or candy to give to kids who came to our 'house,' but we didn't have any money. So Joe had the idea to knock on doors to find out what errand we could do to earn a dollar or two. And this lady had us help her move the garbage cans when we told her what we wanted; and she gave us each a dollar bill."

Grandpa had been prepared to swat the kids and tell them to return the money. Instead, by following the principles in this book, he found he had a creative and practical nine-year-old grandchild he could be proud of — and should encourage.

You can't find or use the best in yourself unless you look for it. You can't find a pattern of meaningful experiences in your life unless you explore for them. You can't find your Motivated Skills, the ones employers are most willing to pay for and the ones that give you greatest personal satisfaction, until you explore certain parts of your life.

Less than a tenth of the skills you have are highly motivated, and mostly they are masked by education, habits, and experience you take for granted. If you are over twenty-one, don't be discouraged by the young adult examples given in this book. Look more deeply to the principles. They are principles being used in many important corporations and government agencies to help people know their skills and get ahead, as well as to assure equal opportunity for all persons regardless of race, sex, origin or age. They also happen to be the principles being used in hundreds of church programs to help men, women and youth become acquainted with their "gifts for ministry," their talents for working in the world "which God so loves."

The bonus is that when you follow the procedures and find the best that is in you, you learn how to have a better life in every way — to find a good job, to help others do the same, and to spread appreciation of each other in a more cooperative and peaceful environment.

Your Future Is Present

1

*"Nothing is so uncommon
as common sense."*
Emerson

"TODAY IS THE FIRST DAY of the rest of your life." You have read that before. But if you want job power, you need to know that an employer can buy only your future, and pay for it on the installment basis by the week or month.

When the employer reads a job application, gives you an interview, inquires about you, he's looking for reliable clues to your future. He's asking in what ways are you likely to be dependable in your performance. All the time the employer is guessing at your future.

You know more than the employer does about yourself. But you have been trained by certain traditions to avoid being aware of the knowledge you have. You have been trained to give limited information about yourself. You have been trained into certain habits of learning that usually hide good opportunities from you, and also prevent employers from using your best skills and talents.

If employers want to use your future, then you need to know which of your skills are likely to help you achieve in the future, help you to grow, help you to enjoy life. When you have that knowledge, you have job power. When you have that knowledge, and can prove your potential, employers often become willing to create opportunities for you

1

—because you are taking most of the guesswork out of hiring.

By the time a young man or woman is eighteen it is possible to identify the pattern of reliable skills that will help you have future achievements, future growth, future fulfillments. [We, the authors, have been helping young and older persons to gain this knowledge and these benefits for more than thirty years, and we have helped many thousands of them.]

From our experiences we can say you must beware of traditional job finding systems and people who endorse them. The old systems are primarily responsible for over 20% unemployment rate among young men and women; for eight million unemployed in 1980; for many millions more who have become discouraged and dropped out of the job market, and countless millions who are frustrated in their jobs. You'll see the evidence of this later.

The time for you to take charge of your future is now. And you can. The steps in this book are simple. They require hard and persevering work for a short time, but it will be worthwhile. A few facts will show why giving that time will be to your advantage. Then you will take the first steps to getting job power now.

Government reports show that in the 1980's most young men and women entering the job market will change jobs 12 to 15 times during their working lives, and change careers possibly five times. A high proportion of these changes will be accompanied by unemployment or time out for retraining and education. And much of that training and education will prepare persons for jobs they neither enjoy nor do very well.

Another fact is that about ten years from now nearly half the working population will be in jobs that have not yet been invented.

These facts about job changing, career changing and

the invention of new types of jobs are important for you to know. They make it clear that traditional job application forms which list education, work history, and experience provide facts that usually mislead employers who are trying to identify a person's potential.

Here are some facts that would ordinarily appear on a job application form that Alice would fill out if she were looking for a job in the traditional way: Work experience—none; hobbies—track; scholastic standing—junior high honors student. That's about it! But our systematic approach reveals that Alice has little time for involvement in anything else, because both her parents work at modest jobs and she cooks dinners for the family of seven—and has done that virtually every day for three years. She plans and organizes meals, schedules her time and the cooking, completes the job daily to the point of washing the dishes and putting them away. On the track team she attends practice daily for two hours, on Saturday three hours, has been on time for more than sixty practices—except for the day she had to take care of a sick sister. In her studies her best subject is English and her compositions are often read to the class. Traditional job application forms and interviews do not invite these other facts. She would be put down as "inexperienced."

Instead of filling out job applications she now gives employers a unique Job Power report, which you will learn in this book to write for yourself. Her Job Power Report says something like this: "I have beginning skills in starting and finishing short-term tasks, being dependably on time, learning quickly, cooperating with other people, following instructions, writing clearly, and planning and organizing my work. I can prove these if you will ask me questions about them."

You know what happened when she showed her Job Power Report to a few people in business? They recommended her for interviews with others, and one of them said: "We don't have a job open right now, but we can find work for someone like you to do until a regular job opens up." A job opening was created there and then because the employer did not have to guess at the skills he was hiring. She made it possible for him to create a job where there was no job. (This book reveals how you can gain the same kind of Job Power.)

Everyone has some kind of excellence, and nearly everyone has what are called hidden talents or skills. Here is another example you will appreciate, even though it is outside your experience. It demonstrates what young persons are up against when looking for jobs. But it comes from a project designed to help older men and women supported by welfare funds, people who hadn't worked in a long time and were in the "dead files" of a State agency as unemployable.

At age 48, Joe Pencil said he had dropped out of high school after one year and worked since then as an exterminator. His last job had ended a year ago. Using the system described in this book we got him to tell us that he "invented a box" that amplified the sounds of termites chewing on woodwork; that he made the first crystal radio set in his home town when he was eight, and then made fifty or sixty more for people who brought him the parts. "They all worked", he said. He could fix any kind of radio, and occasionally made and installed hi-fi sets for friends who would give him a few meals. Then we challenged him on working with TV sets.

"You got me there," he said, "because I can't read and so I can't use the TV manuals. But I do know the insides of six sets; them's what my friends got, and they trust me."

We asked him if he'd like to try for a job as an electronics technician, and he replied: "How could I? I ain't

4

got no experience."

This is a man who worked with electronic systems because he loved doing it, not for pay. And there's no room on job application forms for things you do well because you love doing them. After we trained him how to avoid employment offices, how to create job contacts and how to offer his potential, he got a job in two weeks at double his former rate of pay. Nine months later he'd been given three pay increases, had learned to read and write, and was having a ball at his work as an electronics technician.

These two examples show there is something seriously wrong with traditional systems that prevent people from becoming aware of the skills they already possess, and also make it necessary for employers to guess—and often guess badly—at the skills of job applicants of all ages.

About one person in seven really knows, by age 18, what kind of job or career is right for him or her. The other six needlessly face job frustrations throughout their lives, job frustrations and stresses that lead to sickness and poor productivity—just the things that employers and employees do not want.

Traditional Putdowns For Job Seekers

High school and junior college graduates looking for jobs frequently face this traditional putdown: "You have no experience."

Even if you've never worked for money, that kind of statement is not true. The problem here is how can you relate your studies, your hobbies and sports activities, the things you do at home, with your friends, with a community or church group, or even on your own with the world of work. You've already seen how one student, Alice, overcame this.

"Just fill out our application form, and we'll call you

when something opens up." Variations on that statement include "We don't have anything right now, but if you'll fill out this form Mr. Jones will be glad to interview you." Almost always this is a polite invitation to waste your time filling out a form that ends up in the wastebasket; or waste it plus the time it takes for Mr. Jones to reach the point where he says there aren't many jobs around, but he'll call you when one opens up for a person with your skills.

You've been told many times that you must fill out application forms if you really want to get a job. But it's not true. When you use the systems in this book, you won't fill out another application form or wait for another interview unless there is a job available that will use your unique potential.

By now you're wondering if we are dealing with reality. But after you read about the job finding system given in this book, you'll see that we've got something special going for you—something very different from what you have been taught is possible.

You know that the traditional systems for getting employment are not working for millions of men, women and youth. Here in 1980 nearly 22% of white young men and women and 40% of blacks under 20 are unemployed. Clearly, the traditional system is not working very well, and conditions are worse than they have been for 40 years.

We know what you're up against, because our backgrounds include nontraditional and highly successful education and experience. Of course, we've had the usual kinds of jobs—personnel, religious organization, government, education, big and small industry, professional jobs, general laboring types of work like typing, apple picking, road construction, clearing tables and mopping floors in cafeterias.

We are concerned here with helping you to beat, overcome, get around the traditional obstacles to job

6

finding. You'll find no magic here. Hard and enjoyable work is necessary to make the job finding systems in this book work. You will learn how to unlock your potential, release it from the shackles of traditional thinking in ways that give you power to know your identity and be your real and best self more of the time. You will stop being restricted by antiquated concepts which enable Dr. Margaret Mead to say that people rarely apply more than ten percent of their potential.

When you use the systems in this book a substantial number of persons will want to create job openings for you, and many will. You will also, very likely, become a member of a Job Cooperative—a group of young people who help each other solve job finding and career planning problems. On your own, or with the aid of other Co-op members, you will create an army of job contacts—people who will quietly recommend you for the kinds of jobs you want. And in this Co-op you will practice how to be effective at job interviews, help each other to overcome limitations, even give each other job leads. We'll also be telling you, later, that you should NOT go around asking for a job; but we'll be giving you an effective substitute system.

Your Job Powers

Let's begin the task of identifying your greatest job powers. Okay? Keep in mind that the knowledge you gain will give *you* control of your own growth and development. Sometimes the steps will seem like others you've heard before, but you'll soon find out that they lead to different results. If you're normal you'll resist this work of getting to know yourself; but if you're patient and work at it in several periods you'll find substantial rewards.

You will need to do things on your own, but you will find it very helpful to do many of the tasks in this book

7

with several other young men and women (four or five). If you do it on your own, just work from the book. If you are working with a small group, you will either want a leader to read out the instructions or another book or two—along with large career journal notebooks for writing in.

Because you are looking for strengths within you, you should examine experiences that surely used those strengths. Start thinking of experiences when you feel you did something well that you also enjoyed doing. Call these experiences "Achievements." Remember, an Achievement is something you feel you did well (what counts is your feeling about it, not what you think someone else might have felt), and something you enjoyed doing. It need not be connected with work, though it could be associated with work, hobbies, school, family, social, community or church life, friends, even reading and playing games. In the space that follows, write down the Achievement that first comes to your mind.

Put your age when it happened alongside that experience.

Now remember back as far as you can to another achievement experience. Try to reach back to before you were ten, or even before age five.

Write down two of your earliest achievements in the following spaces, giving your approximate ages at those times.

1.

2.

If you are with a group, stop now and share one of those two earliest achievements. Take turns in saying, in just a few words, what the achievement was.

It is important for you to be aware not only that you achieved something at a very early age—even if it was only the first time you put on your shoes yourself—but also that each other person is an early achiever.

Now, write down an achievement experience you had during the last two or three years, giving your age at that time. Here's space for it.

If you have followed these instructions, you will have stimulated your memory over the range of your life, but with emphasis on special kinds of experiences— Achievements.

We know you have been taught to learn from your mistakes, to find out what you did wrong and "never do that again." What we are aiming at is to help you find out what you did right and enjoyed, so you can identify your own formula to help you have more of *these* experiences.

The next thing to do is to write down short descriptions of a dozen or more Achievement experiences you have had in the spaces that follow. You already have written down a couple you could include, so start by writing them down first. They can be in any order; they do *not* have to be remembered and written down according to your age, and you don't need to list your age at the time of each experience. If you have a little trouble remembering, try to think of a couple for each two or three years of your life—but you'll find they occasionally bunch up in one year or two. Write them down as you think of them; don't worry about how important they might seem to anyone else, because you won't tell others about any you don't want to share. This list is for your private information and learning.

1.

2.

3.

4.

5.

6.

7.

8.

9.

10.

11.

12.

13.

14.

15.

Now you need to go through another kind of choosing process. It will help you to appreciate and understand yourself better. Take your time, and simply place a check against the seven achievements you feel have been most important to you. Make those checks now!

Next, number these seven in order of their importance to you: No. 1 is the Achievement you feel has been of greatest importance of all to you; No. 2 is the one you feel has been of second greatest importance, and so on. When you do it, your mind will be concentrating on what you did on those different occasions, how you did them, what the outcomes were, who—if anyone—was affected besides yourself, where you were, and perhaps why and when. A lot of the detail of those experiences will flow through your mind, and this will help you to perceive some of your dependable strengths, your job powers. As you follow through the steps given, inner strengths you have will become more clear. So now, number those seven checked Achievements in order of their relative importance to you. Later on, if you want to, you can change the numbering, just as you can change the ones you checked originally.

By doing this you are NOT fixing yourself forever. It's as if you are looking at the stars, a compass, and a clock on one of the great oceans to find out where you are at the present moment in your journey. When you know where you are, you are free to change your course. But if you don't know where you are, you cannot know what to steer for; you cannot know how to get to where you want to go.

We said before that you can take the steps given in this book on your own, but that you will find it especially helpful if you are part of a small group. If there are several of you doing this you will finish at different times, but be patient because you will soon be helping each other discover some overlooked skills.

For the next step you will need your Career Journals. As much as possible you want to be able to see *in writing* the skills you used to make each of your top seven Achievements happen. Do this in the order in which you numbered them. Begin with number one, the greatest of all your achievements, and write down what you did to make it happen. What were your activities? Did you read, write, speak, play, run, use tools, travel, relate with someone else, compete, study and take an exam, learn a language? Whatever your activities were, write them down in a description of what you did when you were having that achievement experience. Leave a two-inch margin on the Journal page where you write.

In your Journal, write "Achievement No. 1, Description." Then go on to write the description of what you did to make it happen. Don't give reasons; just write down your activities. When you have done that, go to the next page and do the same for Achievement No. 2, and so on with the other five. You will need about an hour, perhaps longer, so this might be a good time to take a break while you remember about what happened and write down those descriptions. (Members of your group could complete this task at home; but before you break up settle on a time for getting together again. You will need each other at the next meeting.)

At this point we have to give you two sets of instructions. The first is for your small group or Job Cooperative; the second is for you if you are working on your own. In the small group, you will be able to help each other reach out and become aware of more skill areas to explore. You will also get to know each other in a more understanding way, and probably come to have greater respect for each other's uniquenesses and skills.

With a Group

With a felt-tip marker or crayon, write on a large sheet of paper a very brief outline of the top five of your seven greatest Achievements. If you feel that one is too personal to discuss with the others, substitute another top one.

With those Achievement summaries written, decide quickly which one of you will start as Upfronter in the Skills Affirmation process. You will each do it in turn. The Upfronter reads his or her No. 1 Achievement summary, then reads slowly the description given in the Journal. Others listen carefully, and write down on a page (headed by the Upfronter's name) the skills they feel that Achievement experience must have used or applied. The listeners have to guess at these skills, so in part it is a listening and a guessing effort.

If a listener wants more detail in order to be a better guesser at the skills used, the listener asks for more detail: "What did you do to make that happen?" The listener should *not* ask "why" questions. Listeners are trying to "see" the skills used, not trying to "psych-out" the Upfronter.

After each reading of an Achievement description, the Upfronter asks if anyone wants more details. This is necessary because when we write down things for ourselves we frequently use a kind of shorthand that doesn't tell the whole story to another person. The extra bits of information permit the listeners to see more skills, and knowledge of these can be helpful to the Upfronter.

When the Upfronter finishes detailing his five greatest Achievements, listeners take turns in reading off the skills they have written down. Then each one gives that written list to the Upfronter.

The Upfronter thanks them for their work, and comments on how he feels about that Upfront experience.

It is certain that many of the skills written down were used, and also that some errors were made by the others in guessing which skills were used. The Upfronter must later work out which skills were really used. Another thing is sure: listeners are likely to suggest some skills that the Upfronter might have overlooked, and also will not have included some of the skills most obvious to the Upfronter. After all, the listeners are not experts; their special helpfulness is in influencing the Upfronter to do a more careful job of being aware of the skills in his Achievements, and also in affirming him as a specially skilled person— which each person is.

Here are some examples of Achievement experiences, and a few of the skills they show.

(NOTE: Not all skills are listed. Even if you had the same type of experience you could describe it differently and be using different skills.)

Achievement Experience	Some Skills/ Talents Shown
Being a messenger in a hospital. When a nurse or doctor wanted something taken to another part of the hospital or to someone else, I was trusted to get it done.	Reliable person Observant (finds her way around) Memory (remembers what she is told) Physical activity (moves around) Medical environment skill Good with people
Machine operator: ran an electric mimeograph machine. Put the stencil on the drum, stacked the paper right, inked the machine, adjusted it to run straight, then got the job done.	Completes a job given to him Good organizer Neat in arranging things Maybe some mechanical ability (Perhaps independent worker talent)

14

Elected President of class. I talked to other students, won their votes. I said I would help when they had troubles with teachers, and make sure that there was a class dance.	Some leadership talent Some showmanship Talking ability Some salesmanship Good memory Problem solver, maybe Good with people
Twenty-four of my drawings were displayed in a high school exhibit. Some were heads of people and animals, some were sketches of fashions. In color, as well as black and white.	Artistic talent Fashion talent Observant Showmanship Independent worker Color skill
Learning to cook. My first meal was for five of us, and everyone said it was good. I did everything—bought vegetables and meat, prepared and cooked it, set up the table, served everything, and cleaned up afterwards.	Foods talent Neatness Orderly in doing things Finishes the job started Likes to serve others Perhaps some homemaking talent
Teachers' aide. When the teacher was out I kept order in the class. Sometimes I would read to the class. I passed out things and kept the board clean and collected things for the teacher.	Good reader and speaker Showmanship (likes to be in front) Perhaps some leadership Reliable person Neatness
Working in the science lab. Cut up frogs and made slides that I looked at through the microscope. Teacher said I was very good at that.	Skillful with hands Very clean and orderly Color skill (to notice things on slide) Memory (remembered instructions) Patient and careful

15

On Your Own

If you are doing this on your own, you will need to open your notebook to your Greatest Achievement description pages. Start by reading your No. 1 Achievement. Then write down in the two-inch margin the skills you believe you must have used to make it happen. Read the Achievement over again, and try to ask yourself some questions aimed at bringing out more details of what you did—so you can add more skills to your list. Because you are not an expert at this, you will also overlook some of the skills which should be listed. But the tasks given in Chapter Two will help you to be more complete.

Go through the same process with each of the other six—read the Achievement description, write down skills you feel you must have used. Read it again, this time with the idea of trying to ask yourself for more details that could reveal more skills you used. Add those to your list.

This way you end up with seven skills lists.

Now you have started to clarify what's right with you. Perhaps you have begun to see a few skills and conditions that are repeatedly associated with your different Achievements. More clarification is needed, sharper knowledge of your skills pattern must be acquired. Chapter two enables you to have those understandings.

Summary

Let's look at what has happened so far. You (and maybe some friends) have reversed the traditional approach of getting to know yourself. Instead of trying to find out what's wrong with you, so you can avoid repeating mistakes, you have begun to learn what is right with you so you can see how to do things right, in your own way, again and again. Instead of looking for your weaknesses, you have explored experiences to find your strengths, the strengths that can help you overcome and cope with problems. You have begun to get a handle on the skills and talents potential employers are looking for in young men and women.

Unlock
Your Potential

2

> *"Don't believe what your eyes are telling you. All they show is limitation. Look with your understanding, find out what you already know, and you'll see the way to fly."*
> from Jonathan Livingston Seagull

YOU WILL FIND THIS CHAPTER the toughest one in the book. It requires you to do a lot more looking into yourself, as well as some writing about what you see. But you'll find that this new look at yourself reveals diamond-like facets, some of which you had not quite seen before. And the three tasks given in this chapter also permit you to see a little into the future. Because these tasks will bring out the best in yourself you will be able to take possession of your strengths—those that will help you to overcome problems, cope with frustrations, and progress into more and more fulfillments. We're telling you that all this work will prove worthwhile. The examples will show it, but you must test it for yourself.

You are always moving into your potential, you are always growing. When you sharpen your self-understanding you can see more opportunities for yourself—more opportunities to be of service both in your job and in your personal life. The work you do gives you a means of expressing your life and talents, besides providing an income. But you must not let work become an obsession. You can die rich without having lived.

Just that happened to an old man who did let work

become his obsession, his work of making money. He owned a hundred and thirty-two million dollars when he was eighty-seven, and he had outlived all his relatives and college alumni. His life was concentrated on working with financial charts and figures, he spoke with financial experts over the telephone, he rarely left his house. One time he left it and went to a special bank library. He was introduced to files and records on the good works of organizations like the YWCA, YMCA, Boy Scouts, Girls Clubs, religious, educational and public service organizations. He didn't know about any of them, and to avoid taxes his millions had to be given away through his "last will and testament." Obsessed with making money, his living had become empty of friends and life.

The kind of self-knowledge this book gives you will help you to cope with frustrations you cannot entirely avoid. This new form of self-knowledge will enable you to bypass many frustrations, and know a relatively rare form of peacefulness as your life expands.

Only one person in seven knows with reasonable clarity what they want out of life. You can join that rare group when you sharpen and clarify the understanding you have of which skills bring you a sense of fulfillment. One important outcome of this understanding is a greater freedom to choose what you want to do. Learning to use your non-working time to put more life into your living is another important outcome. A third outcome is that you appreciate the difference between Motivated and Unmotivated skills. The Unmotivated ones turn you off sooner or later, even though you have some talent in using them. The Motivated skills, on the other hand, really turn you on when you apply them. Knowledge of which skills are Motivated gives you a handle on how to use them, develop them, train and educate them, combine them in different ways to meet changing job and educational circumstances.

Step 2—Motivated Skills Chart

On the next page is a chart listing separate skills. It has 56 lines, four of them blank. The four lines at the bottom are for you to use when you want to add to the list of 52 skills—perhaps with your own term for some combination of those skills. "Curiosity" is one that some have chosen to add, and "patience" is another sometimes added. The 52 skills in this list can be combined in many ways to fit the requirements of almost all different kinds of jobs.

The usefulness of this chart is that it enables you to look at your greatest achievements to find your Motivated skills, the talents and strengths that they use most often. It will also help you use terms for your skills which relate to jobs, training and continuing education.

Use it this way: Start with your greatest Achievement and slowly go down each item in column 1; make a check against each skill which you feel was *strongly* applied when you were making that achievement happen. You should check at least six, and perhaps ten or more.

Then do the same with Achievement No. 2, making the checkmarks in column 2. Repeat the process for each of the others. Some persons like to number and describe their ten greatest Achievements, so there are ten columns. However, seven will almost always give you a clear indication of the skills most repeatedly used in making the majority of those Achievements happen.

In the last column, total the checkmarks for each skill, then list the skills in order of their number of checks in your Career Journal. This helps clarify which of your Motivated skills are central, most important, to your Achievement pattern.

MOTIVATED SKILLS CHART

INSTRUCTIONS: Start with No. 1 of your seven greatest achievements. In column 1, check off those items strongly applied in your No. 1 achievement. Do the same with achievement No. 2 in column 2, and so on with the others.

COLUMN I

	1	2	3	4	5	6	7	8	9	10	Total
Analysis											
Artistic											
Budgets											
Controls											
Coordination											
Creative											
Design-art											
Details											
Energy-drive											
Economical											
Figures											
Follow-through											
Foresight											
Human relations											
Ideas											
Imagination											
Individualist											
Initiative											
Inventive											
Leader											
Liaison											
Manager											
Mechanical											
Memory											
Negotiations											
Observation											

MOTIVATED SKILLS CHART

INSTRUCTIONS: Start with No. 1 of your seven greatest achievemnets. In column 1, check off those items strongly applied in your No. 1 achievement. Do the same with achievement No. 2 in column 2, and so on with the others.

COLUMN II

	1	2	3	4	5	6	7	8	9	10	Total
Organizer											
Outdoors/travel											
Ownership											
People											
Perceptive											
Persevering											
Personnel											
Persuasive											
Planner											
Policy-making											
Practical											
Problem-solving											
Production											
Programs											
Promotion											
Research											
Sales											
Service											
Showmanship											
Speaking											
Systems/Procedures											
Things											
Training											
Trouble-shooting											
Words											
Writing											

If You're Not Clear

A fair number of young men and women take longer than others to identify their best and Motivated skills and talents. While it is evident that all the self-studying in this chapter must be done individually, it often takes the questioning of another person (or members of a job cooperative) to make that task easier and more complete. The Guidance, Career Development or Placement Counselor in your high school or Community College, especially if trained in the techniques given in this book, can be of help. So can a wise older person with a few years of work experience. (Professional Career counselors trained by Bernard Haldane are in most major cities.) We especially want to recommend the Job Cooperative as a helping source.

If you have difficulty deciding what skills to check in the Motivated Skills Chart, you can ask members of your Co-op group to listen. You describe your No. 1 Achievement, then read out the skills on the chart. The group will suggest items you should check in column No. 1, but you need not accept their ideas; you should let their ideas stimulate your thinking while you make up your own mind on which six or more of the listed skills you should check—the ones that were strongly used to make that experience happen.

You'll never be sure of your future, but that's all you've got ahead of you and that's all an employer wants to hire. So the more keys to it that you have in your possession, the better you'll be able to shape it. The following process will help you to know, and name, the skills most likely to bring you success and fulfillment in the future. You do not know how those skills or talents will be combined in the immediate future, nor the job titles those combinations will have from time to time. Job titles are changing too fast. During the last ten years, for instance, the U.S. Government's *Dictionary of Occupational Titles* shows more than 5,300 jobs were invented or dropped out, some of the new titles being: Opto-mechanical technician, Equal Opportunity representative, Credit card operations manager, Automobile diagnostician, Paramedical assistant, and many in the health, environment and library fields. In addition, the descriptions of many jobs with old titles have changed. But Astronaut and Aquanaut jobs have not yet made it into the Dictionary.

Step 3—Target Your Motivated Skills

This task will help you to see how your skills, talents, strengths relate to a variety of occupations. Complete this task carefully and it will take a lot of guesswork out of your career choice.

A number of skills have been organized into sixteen groupings or clusters that make it easier to relate them to a variety of occupations.

First read over the following list of sixteen skill and activity clusters that combine to make up most jobs:

1. Design, Color, Shape things.
2. Calculate, Count, Keep records.
3. Observe, Operate, Inspect.
4. Write, Read, Talk, Speak, Teach.
5. Hand skills: Fix, Build, Assemble.
6. Analyze, Systematize, Research.
7. Invent, Develop, Create, Imagine.
8. Help people, Be of service, Be kind.
9. Ideas, Beauty, Foresight.
10. Physical, Outdoor, Travel activities.
11. Manage or Direct others.
12. Do Independent work, Own or Collect things.

13. Perform: Music, Acting, Demonstrations.
14. Foods, Cooking, Homemaking.
15. Persuade, Sell, Influence others.
16. Sciences, Engineering.

Now turn to a new page in your Career Journal. Read carefully, again, all sixteen clusters, and write down *the numbers* of four or five that include the skills and activities you feel must be contained in your ideal job or career. Take into account the skills most frequently checked in your chart, and the total of what you have learned so far about yourself through studying your Achievements.

Now look at the first of the clusters you listed. It includes several skills or activities. Write down the one or two items you feel are most important to you, most expressive of you.

Do the same with each of the other clusters you listed.

Now you have listed five to ten of these skills/activities. You next step is making a good guess at which two or three of these are of greatest importance to your life. It will help if you can be in a quiet place for this, so your mind can rest from outside noise. In this quietness let your imagination see yourself doing the most worthwhile and useful thing you can think of. Concentrate on that activity, and perhaps another one like it. Then—after about ten minutes of this quiet awareness—write down those two or three top-value skills/activities. Below them list the others in their approximate order of importance to you.

You now have a list of skills and activities. What follows are descriptions of the sixteen clusters. Begin with your top two or three skills/activities and read their cluster descriptions. Then read the remainder of the cluster descriptions associated with the other skills/activities on your list. Read all those descriptions carefully.

Here are the sixteen cluster descriptions.

1.Design, Color, Shape things. These are commonly associated with artistic qualities, but the man or woman who cuts hair, leather, paper or plastic materials to shapes, or who selects colors that match or contrast, is not an artist in the usual sense.

The surgeon who operates on a patient has to know the shape of the organ and other parts of the body. The architect and engineer must be able to see in their "mind's eye" the shapes they are planning. The pilot must see the shape of the runway to set his plane down right. The bricklayer's ability to erect a straight wall is associated with talent for shaping things. The good dresser has design and color sense.

2. Calculate, Count, Keep Records. This group is concerned with figures and their different applications. The bookkeeper writes down, adds, subtracts and otherwise uses figures; the mathematical researcher has figures as one of his reasoning tools; and the computer programmer works with figures as symbols of simple or complex operations; housewives and other consumers use figures to keep track of grocery money, and grocery clerks use figures to calculate what customers should pay.

3. Observe, Operate, Inspect. Many persons with good eyesight do not see much of what goes on around them. The people who notice everything, who seem to be paying attention all the time, are safe operators of automobiles, airplanes, machines of different kinds. They often are good inspectors, too, if they will concentrate enough. Nurses also need observation skill.

4. Write, Read, Talk, Speak, Teach. All these require the use of words. Everyone uses words, but not everyone would want the use of words to be central to his or her career. The crane operator needs few words, while the news reporter's whole life involves the written or spoken word. Words are important to travel agents, salespersons, inter-

viewers, almost everyone on radio and TV, receptionists, secretaries, most types of executives, all kinds of teachers and trainers, dispatchers, advertising writers, printers, good students, most researchers, writers and public speakers.

5. Handskills: Fix, Build, Assemble. You may have a real knack for doing things with your hands. Some like to work with big things—plumbing, heavy machines, bricks, welding; others might work best with little and light things—woods, plastics, watches, instruments, electronic components. Some like to do this work on their own or for just one or two people at a time, while others would prefer to work in a team or group. It is unusual for the person who likes to work with big and heavy things to also enjoy working with tiny and lightweight things.

This group concerns persons who really like to fix or repair things, build or make things, assemble products of different kinds—and do this work well.

6. Analyze, Systematize, Research. These are the problem-solving, planning, research and organizing skills. People with these skills want to know the "why" of things, and often the "how" of things. Analysts tend to break things down into parts; sometimes they observe the parts and organize them into smoothly flowing operations—as systematizers.

Researchers may be analytical, yet they sometimes are systematizers; they certainly aid both. And while the researchers usually work on their own, it is becoming more commonplace for them to work in small teams.

All planning is associated with analysis and research whether the planning involves a budget, a career, a corporation or a government forecast. Jobs associated with group No. 6 nearly always require considerable formal education or study.

7. Invent, Develop, Create, Imagine. New products,

new ideas, and adaptations of products and ideas—these changes are happening all the time in all parts of the world. There is constant demand for creative people, those who originate and modify for the better whatever exists materially and in the mind.

There are little changes and big ones. Someone thought up the idea of putting ridges on paper clips; someone dreamed up the idea of the ceramic nose cone which permits re-entry of rockets coming back to earth; someone worked out how to transplant human organs.

Creativity, imagination, inventiveness, adaptation—all are parts of progress in every occupation. These qualities often are needed to help find the right solution to problems in human relations as well as in scientific, technical and management fields.

8. Help People, Be of Service, Be Kind. The human relations occupations are associated with these. They are needed in different degrees by nurses, interviewers, receptionists, social workers, teachers, clergymen, hotel and restaurant hostesses and head waiters, social anthropologists, politicians, some psychologists and doctors, recreation directors, many lawyers, counselors, and others whose work or business requires them to be dependent on people relationships. Enthusiasm, trust in others, patience with others—all are elements of this group.

Those strong in this group must be willing to be of service to people they want to organize or lead. Many managers and executives are said to be effective because they are willing to be of service. In these areas many new types of occupations are opening up.

9. Ideas, Beauty, Foresight. This group often is associated with No. 7, sometimes with No. 6, and is also associated with beauty and harmony of life. Dealers in antique furniture, museum curators, others who have appreciation for the greatness of life everywhere are likely to

have checked this one. Farsighted business leaders and diplomats, outstanding men and women in the advertising field, as well as many of the creative persons concerned with futuristics are likely to recognize strength in this group. Many young men and women have demonstrated talent along these lines through actions that required anticipating future events and planning for them with sensitivity.

10. Physical, Outdoor, Travel Activities. Sports and athletics are not the only careers associated with this group. It also includes the physical movement of people and things; so it includes the truck driver, the world traveler, the ballerina. Some others are recreation directors, most people in the construction industry, traffic managers, travel agents, many types of entertainers who must be on their feet for long periods.

Civil engineers work on outdoor piping, bridges, dams, and other structures; geologists and mining engineers, miners, airline stewards, pilots, all are concerned with the movement of things and people, and to this extent all are concerned with group No. 10.

11. Manage or Direct others. This is the leadership group. Check this only if you really have experience being the boss or leader of a group, association, club, team, etc.

This type of person is formally or informally elected to head up an activity of some kind. It could be to head up a student group or to direct something in a community. Three or more of these leadership experiences, ones which include managing others, indicate real strength in this group. While many persons dream of being great leaders, the concern here is with actual leadership—if only on a small scale.

12. Independent Work, Own or Collect Things. People who want to run their own businesses, including doctors and other professional persons, should check this

one. There are many independent workers—individual researchers and inventors, independent consultants, plumbers who work alone, and other "loner" types who will also want to check this.

One of the main differences between the independent employee and the successful small business owner is the way they think. The owner tends to think about "my property, my collection, the things I own." He is sensitive to accumulating things, including money with which to buy things as an owner. Others who do not feel the same way (most of us) do not take the trouble to learn how to collect things—including bills. (Most independent doctors, for instance, employ professional bill collectors and business managers.)

13. Perform: Music, Acting, Demonstrations. Shakespeare said we all are players on the world's stage. Many of us are not good at getting up before people; others are ham actors, and a few are really good performers. But there are many varieties of performing, most of which does not take place on a regular stage. Just being well dressed, or the deliberate opposite, is one kind of performance. Demonstrators in stores need a kind of performing ability. Receptionists in offices and showrooms need showmanship to enjoy their work; so must professional hosts and hostesses. Public speakers and politicians have to put on a show. The best teachers use showmanship in their work.

Let your Achievement facts, not your dreams, reveal if you should check this group. There is no doubt about actors, actresses, musicians; no doubt about twirlers, majorettes, elected class presidents, or athletes who love to see their pictures in the papers.

14. Foods, Cooking, Homemaking. If your greatest achievements include cooking, homecare, babysitting, this is one of the groups you should have checked. Clarence Birdseye, who invented the frozen food process, was proud

of the fact that he was the only boy in his high school cooking class. And a White House pastry cook was very happy to tell about his first success in baking pastry at the age of seven. (Many women overlook the fact that excellent home-making usually applies group 6 items as well as group 3 items.)

15. Persuade, Sell, Influence Others. It is obvious that the salesman should check here. Not so obvious is the student negotiator who influences a college or high school administration to change a rule. Included here is the person from whom others regularly seek advice, the business manager, the peacemaker between conflicting groups and individuals, the scientist or other employee who sells an idea up the line, the "smoothie" who has a knack for conning others.

The persuasive arts extend to the diplomat, the clergyman, many teachers, training directors, business negotiators, politicians of all kinds, public relations counselors, lobbyists, advertising executives, a host of persuaders running from the corner peddler to executives who negotiate multimillion dollar deals.

16. Sciences, Engineering. Education in these fields offers the best formal training available in the art of thinking for yourself. Some scientists and engineers are concerned with making better use of today's facts. These are applied scientists (they range from architect and atomic scientist to the zoologist.) In most branches of science and engineering there are specialists and subspecialists. The men and women in applied sciences usually work on ways to improve the applications of present knowledge. The "pure" scientists and engineers usually are the seekers of new knowledge, new types of information, "new" natural laws.

When you read the cluster descriptions in this way you

will almost certainly find expanded possibilities for application of your list of skills/activities. So now you should turn to your Journal, write the title "Ideal Job/Career Description," and write under it the activities you feel will combine to make up your "ideal" job. That is your target. But be sure to take into consideration the increasing number of paraprofessional jobs that are growing fast; these include paramedics, paralegal jobs and teacher's aide occupations.

You have now studied your greatest Achievements three times, each from a different viewpoint. First in Chapter 1 when you guessed at your related skills; second when you charted your Motivated skills; third, as you related these skills to the 16 clusters. Each time you probably noticed different things about yourself—with some increasing in importance and others decreasing. Our purpose is to get the best of you into the open and in focus, so that key elements in your fulfilling future can become clearer.

Two case histories will show how the Motivated skills chart works and how Step No. 3, Target Your Motivated Skills, helps to clarify job goals.

Hank Wilson, age 18, ran away from home when he was 15 and stayed away for several weeks, supporting himself by repairing motorbikes and doing odd jobs. Then he went home, graduated from high school, started college, quit and volunteered for military service. His top five achievements were these:

"Achievement No. 1: At age 14, restored and remodeled a neighbor's cottage so well that lots of jobs like it were offered to me and filled all my spare time during the school year. That summer I operated several pieces of gardening equipment and worked for the customers of a professional gardener. I kept the equipment in good repair, and got along well with the customers.

"Achievement No. 2: I started living on a dairy farm when I was nine and for the next five years learned every part of how to run it. By the time I was 14 I kept the records, bought equipment and feed, sold the milk, hay and meat, maintained and repaired the equipment, did necessary carpentry, supervised and paid a grownup helper, and turned in a small profit.

"Achievement No. 3: At fifteen I left home and hitch-hiked twelve hundred miles. I wanted to be completely independent, because I already had done many things successfully that lots of grownups weren't capable of doing. I got a job as a mechanic in a motorcycle shop. During those five weeks I grew up more and learned more than at any other time in my life. I wasn't comfortable when I came back home, and felt guilty about my parents supporting me while I was in high school.

"Achievement No. 4: I was elected president of the student body at grammar school when I was twelve, and the faculty picked me to be patrol leader.

"Achievement No. 5: My first term in college I received bids to join 12 fraternities. This is a sign of great popularity, but it was one of the unhappiest times in my life and my grades were terrible. I couldn't see where being in college was helping me."

Of the sixteen skill clusters, Hank checked numbers 3, 4, 5, 10, 11, 12 and 15—more than the four or five requested. Then he chose these top-value activities: independent work, outdoors or travel activities, speak-teach, sell-persuade, fix-build-assemble, help people, manage.

After he studied the cluster descriptions he wrote down under "Ideal Job/Career Description," salesman of heavy equipment, explaining and demonstrating it to customers.

"This would be independent and outdoor work; it would involve speaking, teaching, selling, occasional fixing, and helping people. I could be a manager when I learned the business," he wrote.

When he came for job counseling, Hank was very confused and felt he was a failure. His popularity was good, but his college work was bad, and that was a very new experience for him. And when he dropped out, he hadn't tried to support himself as he had at age 15. He felt he had escaped into a soft military job, which in a couple of months had frustrated and failed to challenge him. He couldn't get out of that job. He needed to feel useful again, and be able to look ahead to something constructive.

By the time he had written his "Ideal Job Description" he had regained his self-confidence and was prepared to make the most of his military assignment, particularly as it related to developing his leadership skills and working with heavy equipment. And he was thinking about taking all the study courses he could, courses for which he might later get college credits.

We'll get back to Hank again when we get into the Reality Test, and again in the next chapter on the Job Power Report.

Phyllis Alison, age 19, is unique in a different way. She is in college, and these are her top five achievements:

"Achievement No. 1: I won many ribbons in horse shows, each time giving many months to perfecting my own riding and the performance and appearance of the horse.

"Achievement No. 2: Working as waitress at parties for a fancy caterer gave me a feeling of what it's like to work under pressure—setting up for parties in a limited time, being part of a team, working with people.

"Achievement No. 3: The unpleasantness of my job in a donut shop makes this important. The conditions were adverse and the pressure was very great.

"Achievement No. 4: Going to Argentina with a friend who spoke no Spanish enabled me to practice my Spanish. Flying by myself and being away from my parents for a long time was a new experience.

"Achievement No. 5: I worked on a high school literary magazine and found out how much work is required to put it together and edit the material."

Oddly enough, she rated only as Achievement No. 7 her membership in a high school honor society. This seems to suggest a sexist influence because her 3.95 academic average (out of 4.00) indicates high intellect, yet she rated her brainpower below babysitting and donut serving. That influence makes it harder to be clear about items in the sixteen clusters of skills. These are the ones she listed: Read (4), Outdoor/travel (10), Independent work (12), Be of service (8), Foods (14), and Manage (11).

After she explored the skill-cluster descriptions she came up with the thought that she would like to work with flowers or other natural things, study them, work out ways to make her information useful to people, and perhaps also be involved with food in some way. She asked questions about the National Park Service, and is planning to explore possibilities with the U.S. Department of Agriculture before deciding on her college major.

These two examples show that when facts are viewed through traditional lenses of *total* history and work experience a clear picture usually does not emerge. But when historical facts are *selected* on the basis of experiences that include doing things well and feelings of achievement, they show much more.

As the Bible urges, people should let their light shine, let their good works be known, speak about that which is good, avoid hiding their light under a bushel.

But we must get into the reality of things. You don't want to be accused of doing a "snow job" with an employer. The Reality Test takes care of that and it also makes sure you don't fool yourself.

Step 4—Reality Test

You may feel you can skip this, and some people do. But this test prepares you for your job interviews, gives you clear facts to put into your Job Power Report, and also makes sure your feet are on the ground when you look for your job and plan for further education and training.

First, ask yourself what kinds of activities you want in your ideal job, and write them in your Career Journal under the heading Reality Test. Hank, for example, said he wanted these things: demonstrating and selling heavy equipment, working outdoors with some travel, equipment maintenance and repair, socializing with people, doing something competitive, and later being a leader or manager.

Then, at the top of a fresh page in your Career Journal, write one of those activities. Write under it details about two or more things you have done along those lines. The details should show your best effectiveness in relation to the activity. Do the same for each of your "Ideal Job" activities, writing each one at the top of a fresh page in your Career Journal, and writing underneath it experiences that demonstrate that activity or one similar to it.

After you complete these descriptions, read them through and then try to describe again (without referring back) the activities you feel you can do well in a job ideally suited to you.

Take a look at what Hank did. He could realistically write these examples under SELLING. "Rebuilt, restored and sold a 1949 Pontiac when I was eleven. Also, built up a paper route over three years starting at age 8; electioneered and won student body presidency in grammar school; sold

37

dairy products at a profit for more than five years; elected president of church Youth Fellowship; completely built (and sold) a trophy-winning hot rod; repaired and sold several old cars when I was 15 and 16. Member of the high school debating team."

On a new page, under DEMONSTRATING HEAVY EQUIPMENT, he wrote these related experiences: "More than eight years experience in operating both small and large farm equipment and machinery including tractors, harvesters, milking machines; also repaired and maintained them. I quickly learn how things work, and can show people how to use them; I trained three helpers."

On a third page of his Journal, under EQUIPMENT MAINTENANCE AND REPAIR he wrote these things: "I've been fixing things ever since I was five, when I successfully repaired a toaster, an iron, and took apart and repaired an alarm clock. I could fix anything on my bike since I was seven, worked as mechanic with a motorcycle repair shop, restored many junked and old automobile engines, built a hot rod which won a trophy; maintained and fixed most kinds of farm and garden equipment and machinery; as carpenter and construction worker, personally remodeled a cottage and filled requests for different construction work which required careful handyman skills."

Hank wrote a lot more on different activities, but these three enable us to explain the value and usefulness of the Reality Test process.

You will note that some of the examples he gave did not come from his Greatest Achievement descriptions. They did come from many of the achievements he recorded in his Career Journal, as well as from other experiences he remembered. This Reality Test section is designed to pull together all your experiences, all those that can be used to support a special area of activity. Even his alarm clock as-

38

sembly when he was five is included, because it helps Hank to know that his skill in maintenance and repair work goes back more than twelve years. With that kind of knowledge, he is aware that this Maintenance and Repair skill is a possession that is never likely to leave him, that is always ready to be applied in doing a dependable job.

Hank's examples alsc show that everything *related* to an activity, even if it has been said in a different context under another activity, should be written down. For instance, the last item under SELLING is "member of the debating team." That same item should also be written under the TALKING TO GROUPS activity. You are not trying to do a snow job on yourself. What you are doing is proving in the strongest possible way that you have potential in that kind of activity. It's your future potential that you are seeking to demonstrate.

In this Reality Test process you either prove you have potential in an activity area, or you must take it out of your present career thinking. If you are weak in your evidence or proof, then you know you must have more training or education in it or stop kidding yourself about its dependability.

Most young persons do not have the concrete evidence shown by Hank's experiences, except in one or two areas. Don't let that worry you. Hank's case makes several points, and it especially shows that each person does have some kind of excellence, even someone who runs away from home when he's fifteen, and drops out of college after one term.

Another thing you learn from the Reality Test is what things you can talk about and what things you shouldn't talk about at job interviews. You should talk about those things you can prove you have potential for; you should not talk about things you cannot prove. But you don't have to give every bit of detail, as you will see in the Job Power Report chapter, which follows. At an interview you should give *enough* proof that you have potential in an activity or skill area, but you must be careful not to overdo it. What you say must be believable. For instance Hank, at age 18, could say he had more than twelve years of experience in repairing and maintaining mechanical and electrical machines and equipment. That would be true, but he would not be believed. And nothing he said after that would be believed.

Summary

This has been a tough chapter to work through, partly because hardly any of us wants the responsibility of really knowing the best that is in us. But unless you do know your best and motivated skills and talents, you can hardly expect to find fulfillment and satisfying growth. So the tasks here involved making a chart which shows those skills that are most often repeated in your greatest achievements; then studying them some more in the light of short descriptions of the kinds of activities and careers they relate to. The third task was a Reality Test which enabled you to prove how strongly you can support the potential you claim to have. This Reality Test shows how strong or weak your proof is, and in this way enables you to avoid some of the mistakes people make by looking for jobs that fail to use the best that is in them.

Job
Power
Tool

3

TOOLS ARE SUPPOSED to make work easier. The best tool you can have when you are looking for a job is a Job Power Report.

Your Job Power Report, done right and used right, keeps you from forgetting anything of importance at a job interview. It influences employers to ask questions that help you put your best foot forward. It saves you lots of time when answering advertisements. It almost eliminates the need to fill out job application forms. It enables you to practice what you want to say at job interviews, which will make you much less nervous. It helps you to get interviews without turndowns (which you'll learn to do in Chapter Four).

One of the most important things the Job Power Report does is help you overcome the attitudes of older persons who believe that young job seekers have no experience and virtually nothing to offer an employer.

If you completed the tasks given in previous chapters, you have already done the basic work needed to make your Job Power Report. You have studied your greatest Achievements, checked them on the skills chart, and used the

Reality Test to make sure you have the skills and activities that fit into your ideal job.

When you job hunt you are constantly in a crisis situation. You are meeting new people at interviews. You are trying to enter a new part of the world—the world of work. And you are moving away from the very sheltered world of education. In the working world you will be meeting people similar to those you've met before, but their attitudes will often be very different. Their actions and manner of speech will be very different. Even if you have worked part-time while in school, and have some acquaintance with the working world, the thought of entering it on a full-time basis can be scary.

You don't want employers to treat you like a kid. But you are not sure what you should do if that happens. You're probably not clear about what job you should ask for. You don't know how interviewers want you to answer their questions, nor what questions they'll ask. You don't know how much time you'll have at interviews, nor if you'll be able to correct mistakes you might make. You probably don't know how to fill out a job application form, especially if you're asked to do it in a hurry. You don't know how to get contacts and job leads, except perhaps through public employment services, private agencies, and maybe your friends or family.

When you have your Job Power Report, all these fears and unknowns will be greatly lessened.

Here is a Job Power Report you can study. This one was used by a young woman looking for a summer job. Your report is sure to be different, but the principles that go into developing it will be the same.

```
JOB POWER REPORT OF................Janis B. Ronay
                                    214 North Street
                                    Atlanta, Ga. 19620
                                    Tel: 123-4566

Skills I
Can Offer:       Perserverance and reliability, quick
                 learning ability, cool in emergen-
                 cies, good memory, good spelling,
                 keep things in order, good listener
                 and follower of instructions, lead-
                 ership, competitive, persuasive,
                 good finger-skills.  These are be-
                 ginning skills.

PROOF:           Elected President of Y-Teens (YWCA)
                 on basis of ability and example:
                 also elected President of Glee Club;
                 organized their many events and ac-
                 tivities ..... Sold jewelry through
                 fashion parties ... In top academic
                 group of my class ... Selected to be
                 in both the Atlanta Chorus and the
                 State Chorus ... Make clothes for
                 myself and for others who pay me
                 for it.

Personal:        Age 16, 5'3", 126 lbs.
```

Janis wrote an effective Job Power Report. Let's see why it is a good job finding tool:

1. There is no statement about what kind of job she wants. Yet you've been told a dozen times that you must decide on what job you want. See why we say you don't need to, and make up your own mind which way makes more sense. About 2,500 of the approximately 25,000 different jobs that exist are changing every year—some dying, some changing in content, some new ones being added. You cannot possibly know which ones have changed or are changing right now. That's one reason why you shouldn't use a job title, unless you are the one person in seven who really has a "fix" on his or her career. Another reason is that the same job titles often mean different duties in dif-

ferent organizations. A third reason is that you want to have the best opportunity to use and develop your skills, and putting a title on them is more likely to limit than to increase that opportunity. A fourth reason is that by leaving a job title off your report, you get the interviewer involved in asking just what you do want. Your Job Power Report must be a tool for getting people interested in you. The more involved they become, the more effective your tool. If you are clear about the job title you want, then you certainly should state it. Beware of indicating that you are expert (unless you really are). Even where you are expert, be sure you make it clear that you have limited experience, which is always true of young men and women.

You might want to try using two different job titles. For instance, someone who has bought junkyard cars, fixed them up and sold them, and loves to do that, might aim one Job Power Report at auto mechanics, and the other at technical sales. In the first case he might start his Report with: "Automobile Mechanic—good at fixing car engines, can hear where the trouble is and make needed adjustments or repairs so it runs well again; mostly experienced with Ford, Chevy and VW engines; trained by first class mechanics who showed me and told me things, and also by experience in salvaging junked cars, repairing them and selling five of them. At age 18 I still have a lot to learn, but I learn mechanical things quickly." The technical or mechanical sales Report would be written so as to emphasize the selling skill.

If you are going to start with a job title, you need to find out its general meaning. You can do that in one of two ways: ask a librarian, or a vocational guidance counselor, to show you a book about the kind of job you want. The U.S. Department of Labor (Washington D.C. 20213) puts out little books, sometimes chapters in larger books, on many kinds of jobs. One way, in other words, is to read

44

about it in order to find out which of your skills really relate to that job. Another way of getting a clear idea of what specific job titles entail is to ask two or three people doing that kind of work. If you take this second way, you will be in contact with persons who could later help you to get job leads (see Chapter 4).

2. The "Skills I Can Offer" paragraph is a simple listing of the skills and talents you have proven by following the steps given in Chapters 1 and 2. They can be organized in one of two ways: either beginning with the top abilities you can prove, qualities you feel an employer wants (as in Janis's Job Power Report); or beginning with the skills that are central to what you want to do, as with the one that begins, "Auto Mechanic—good at fixing car engines."

To see what we mean by "skills that are central", think about a truck driver, a scientific researcher, and a newspaper reporter. All of them must be observant, and this is sure to be among their top skills. But being observant is essential and central to being a truck driver; being analytical is more important to a researcher; and writing skill is more important to a newspaper reporter. You worked out your central skills when you studied the sixteen work areas in the previous chapter and when you used the Skills Chart and the Reality Test.

Never list your skills in alphabetical order, as you might be tempted to do, because this could give the wrong impression to an employer. For instance, if you are *accurate* in keeping records, have a good *memory*, are very *observant*, *safety conscious*, and love to *travel*, you might be offered a warehouse record-keeping job. But if you put "very observant and safety conscious" first, the opportunity to drive a truck might be offered.

When you've written your "Skills I Can Offer" section, it might seem as though you have a very great deal to offer, and some persons will suggest that it sounds like bragging.

Do keep in mind that yours are not fully-developed skills, they are beginning skills, living and growing skills which you can prove you possess. And the proof you offer shows the level to which they have been developed. So you're not fooling anyone. You certainly should not let anyone get away with the idea that you have nothing at all to offer, just because you may not have worked for pay before. However, be sure that you can support with examples your good potential for each skill included in this paragraph.

3. The "Proof" paragraph is optional, though most people do use it. If you do not use it, write something like this in its place: "Please ask me questions about any of these skills." When you do use this paragraph, be sure you are careful to give examples that show your highest level of effectiveness in the different skills, and indicate that there are other examples you could give. A phrase like this could be used: "Some of the experiences that demonstrate I have these skills include:" Then you could give a brief statement of some of those experiences.

Don't say too much in this section. The person looking at it should be able to read your complete Job Power Report in about 45 to 90 seconds—less than two minutes—which means less than 200 words for both paragraphs.

4. Always include your age and something descriptive. like height and weight. If your schooling facts are to your advantage, include them. If you are in a wheelchair, blind, or otherwise what some people call "handicapped," do not mention these in your Report. But be prepared to talk about your situation as soon as you get your inter-views—perhaps along these lines if you are in a wheelchair: "Thank you for seeing me Mr. Jones. The skills shown in this Job Power Report (hand it to him) are not limited by my being in a wheelchair. Will you please ask me some questions about them?" Or, if you are blind you might say: "The skills I have listed are sometimes strengthened be-

cause of my blindness." Or if you are deaf, you might be able to say: "One of my special assets is that it doesn't bother me to work in noisy places because I'm deaf." More importantly, if you are "handicapped," take advantage of the excellent assistance offered through your State Rehabilitation Service. Throughout the country, nearly all of its employees do very fine work helping their clients to get jobs.

5. Your name and address should be in the upper right part of the Job Power Report. Always include a telephone number where you can be reached, or where you will get a message. A group or Job Cooperative can be useful by providing a central number through which those without telephones can be reached. In the working world, decisions about employing someone are often followed by a telephone call, so you need to let it be known that you can be reached through a certain telephone number. But if it is not your own, you should say so at the interview, perhaps along these lines: "I'm sure you can leave a message for me at the phone number listed in my Job Power Report. I'm over there just about every day, and they know where to reach me in the next block."

6. If you have work history, it is usually advisable to leave it out *unless* it supports what you say in the "Skills I Offer" paragraph. Most older persons include work history in what is called a resume (something like a Job Power Report), but an obituary-like chronological listing of jobs usually buries the person's skills. As you know, a lot of young men and women take on jobs to make a buck, and they go for the ones that pay the most. That doesn't mean they enjoy those jobs, or even do them well. Occasionally someone of sixteen will lie about his age and get a construction job paying about six dollars an hour—which is at the rate of $11,000 a year. But what he or she could really be

working at is getting the cash needed for down payment on a car.

The rule here is that you do not put into your Job Power Report anything which might mislead an employer or alert him to skills that you don't enjoy using.

For instance, if you did work on a construction job for the money, and you did not include it in your Report, here is how you could talk about it at an interview: "I'm willing to work hard for what I want, and one of my skills is driving safely. So even though I don't like construction laboring, I figured out it was the best paying job around and doing that kind of work would quickly let me save money for a down payment on a car."

When you say it that way, it affirms your practicality as well as your safe driving skill, and it takes away from the interviewer the weight he might give to your mention of working as a construction laborer. An oversimplification of the rule is, if you don't want to do it again, don't put it in your report.

Now we'll get to a list of what you'll need to prepare your Job Power Report, and then give you several Report examples. The things you'll need from your Career Journal to prepare your Job Power Report are:

1. The list of your strongest or motivated skills

2. Your Motivated Skills Chart

3. Your Reality Test pages detailing experiences that demonstrate your effectiveness in different activities

4. A list of your education, training, work experiences and social and family activities that could give evidence of any of your skills or talents.

The following steps will help you prepare your Job Power Report:

1. Write "JOB POWER REPORT OF . . . " on the left near the top of a sheet of paper about 5.5x8.5 inches. On the right put your name, address and phone number.

2. Above the middle of the page write down the skills you have proved through your Reality Test pages, and the activities with which they are related. Be sure you put first either those attitudes and activities that you feel sure will give a favorable impression, or especially strong skills that you don't ever want to be overlooked. (You will see in the examples how this is done.)

3. In a second paragraph, again using your Reality Test facts, summarize—in as few words as possible—those experiences that demonstrate the skills given in your first paragraph.

4. If these two paragraphs total more than 200 or less than 90 words, edit them (or get help in doing that) so your Job Power Report can be read by an interviewer in 45 to 90 seconds.

5. Your "Personal" section can also include your work history if there is any. Include your age, your schooling and class standing if these will be helpful (otherwise leave them out), your height and weight. When you do include a work history, keep it very brief.

The facts about yourself may require you to modify some of these steps, but for the great majority of young men and women between 16 and 21 these five steps will result in an effective Job Power Report.

If your spelling or writing abilities are not too good, develop your Report and then get someone who can spell and write to fix it up in final shape. (This is another place when members of your small group or Job Cooperative can be helpful.)

The following nine samples demonstrate different styles of Job Power Reports, and some before and after problems. The first one is that of Jeannie Gibbs.

JOB POWER REPORT OF..................JEANNIE GIBBS
                                       193-17 56th Avenue
                             Lindenhurst, N.Y.   19116
                             Tel: 461-1191

Artist, exhibitor, prizewinner. Careful young
artist with portfolio of fashion, people, animals.
More than five years of training have developed
talent shown since early childhood. Top student
in art class. Studied techniques of commercial
artists and fashion designers. More than twenty
of my pictures were used to decorate high school
art rooms.

I also write well, and collaborated in writing a
short story. But art is my life, and I continue
to listen, observe and learn. My age is seventeen.

Would you like to see my portfolio, and ask me
some questions?

Before you say, "What's so unusual about that for someone who won an art competition," take some other facts into consideration. She was a delinquent who had been "away" for six months; she was afraid to look for a job; she acted very shy and had almost no self-confidence when she joined our Job Cooperative. At the beginning she said she had no achievements she could remember; with some encouragement, from seventeen others in the Co-op, she began to write down achievements and soon was in the swing of the self-discovery activities described in Chapters One and Two. She practiced talking about her drawings, paintings and other achievements, and her self-confidence returned.

She applied our techniques for getting interviews, and was recommended from one person to another. After being interviewed twenty times without getting turned down, she got the kind of job she wanted as Assistant to a commercial artist—in two weeks. She had been without a job, feeling more and more hopeless, for over two months.

50

Barry's achievements are different. Look at them, think about what skills you could find in them, and what kind of job Barry would be offered before he went through the tasks described in earlier Chapters 1 and 2.

At first, he denied that he had any skills, and it was hard to get him to stay with the Job Co-op. His greatest achievement, he said, was finding out "that he knew he could play sports half way decent (basketball, baseball, football). No. 2—Cutting grass. No. 3—Learning about myself. No. 4—Learning all about sex, girls, etc. No. 5—Driving and learning about cars. No. 6—Learning how to play the accordion. No. 7—Riding a bike. No. 8—Refinishing furniture."

By the time he completed his Reality Test, and talked about his best talents with other members of the Co-op, Barry realized that the skills he used to play the accordion, to fix cars and his bike were all hand skills. When he was playing softly on his accordion, his light touch and movements were not very different in quality from those he used to finish furniture. He discovered that being pleased with the attention he got from being on the athletic field was similar to the feeling he got when people responded to his accordion playing. It takes good observation and a good sense of physical and spatial balance to be on three athletic teams, to drive a car safely and to ride a bike well.

These are the key paragraphs in his Job Power Report:

```
Skills I
Can Offer:      Very observant, good sense of how
                things fit together and how to fix
                them, willing to work where I can
                be seen, good physical endurance
                and strength, patient in learning
                and quick in what I do, safe driver.

PROOF:          Letters in basketball, baseball, and
                football; good driver, no accidents
                in two years; bought my car with
```

money earned fixing cars for friends,
neighbors and others, by contracting
to cut grass, and sometimes playing
accordion in a band.

Personal: Age 18, high school graduate.

Barry was pleased with his Job Power Report. But he
was skeptical that it could be helpful. So on his way home
when he stopped off for gas, he called to the station
manager and said, "Hey, will you take a minute to look at
this and tell me if you think it could help me get a job? I'm
not asking you for one, and I don't expect you to know of
one."

The station manager came over, quickly read it, asked
Barry a couple of questions and said, "We're shorthanded
here evenings and weekends. If you'd like to try it out I'd
like to have someone like you working for me."

Barry turned his car around and came right back to
the Church where his Job Co-op was and told the priest his
experience. He'd told the manager he'd think about it and
let him know in a couple of days. But Barry had found out
that the system in this book could work for him, so he made
it work some more and got the different job that he wanted.

Here's another one:

JOB POWER REPORT OF ... .MERRY LOVE
                        143 Omega Street S.E.
                        Lincoln, Neb.   41565
                        TEL: 123-4567

Skills I
Can Offer: Patient, helpful with people problems,
             calm in emergencies, careful and pre-
             cise handskills, good intelligence.

PROOF: Biology dissections and related
             tests - top grade in class; invited
             back two summers to work again with

disabled children; always being asked
to help friends with their school
work and personal problems; babysitting work pays for my clothes; I
play the guitar and piano; when my
parents get emotionally upset I am
able to calm them down. Candystriper.

Personal: Age 18. High school graduate, Jan.,1976

Merry's information was developed from beginning with these top achievements: 1. Calming down my parents when they're emotionally upset, 2. Working with disabled children, 3. Helping my friends with their problems and their school work, 4. Learning to play guitar and piano, 5. Paying for my clothes with babysitting money, 6. Planting flowers and helping them grow, 7. Helping my parents around the house.

You remember Hank Wilson. His greatest achievements were listed in Chapter 2 in relation to skill clusters and the Reality Test. He's the one who left home when he was fifteen, repaired motorbikes, went back home, graduated from high school and left college after one term. One reason he wanted a Job Power Report was that once he wrote one he felt he could change it from time to time as he gained experience and education in the Air Force. Six months before his term was up, he decided he could begin to make job contacts in the civilian working world. Here is his Job Power Report at age 18.

JOB POWER REPORT OF ...... HENRY (HANK) J. WILSON
                          119 Fort McHenry Drive
                          Jamestown, Va.   22613
                          Tel: 119-3168

Skills I
Possess: Communicate well, several handskills
             (cars, bricklaying, carpentry, cement/
             plastering, farm machinery, etc.),
             good with people of all ages, lead-
             ership, start and finish things on
             my own as well as with a team, very

53

```
                    observant, good memory, like being
                    outdoors and traveling.  Very per-
                    suasive.

Evidence:           Elected president of two student
                    bodies; repaired and refinished
                    houses, added rooms, sold my services;
                    fixed, sold and made a profit on two
                    old cars; employed as motorcycle
                    mechanic; managed a small firm with
                    two helpers:  purchased supplies and
                    equipment, buildings, kept all re-
                    cords, sold produce and milk, made
                    a small profit.  I know that's a lot
                    to believe about a young man of 18,
                    but you can ask me questions about it.

Personal:    6'2", excellent health, some college.
```

"There's no room for this kind of information on a job application form", Hank said. "It all sounds impressive, and yet it's true. I'd like to try it out now, just to see how people react to it."

Our counselor said, "It might even have some influence on your Air Force job. Maybe you should check it with your commanding officer and ask him if he thinks it's the kind of thing that would help you get a job outside."

Well, that's what he did. And the result was that after interviews with several officers, he was sent back to college at government expense and agreed to continue in the Air Force for a couple of years after that, meanwhile keeping up with his military training.

In one of Bernard Haldane's Career Planning courses at Fairleigh-Dickinson University, one freshman student had been counseled through the Admissions Office to take engineering courses because his math was so good. His Greatest Achievements list showed he had organized three dance bands, managed them and kept them busy with bookings through two summers and Saturday nights most of two school years. He made enough money then to pay his own way for three years of college. He was a trumpet player himself. He had so much fun with those activities that he didn't relate them to a career possibility. He knew he worked hard to get those bookings, but he had enjoyed that, too. Just before he wrote his Job Power Report, he arranged to switch to business management and marketing or selling courses.

A well-meaning relative had told him that when he went to college he would have to stop playing around. So he was prepared to drop the activities that the Career Planning course made clear were the essence of his life. Here is the first paragraph of his Report. He was not yet eighteen.

```
Skills I
Can Prove:      Business management, sales and or-
                ganizing skills, associated with
                dance bands and entertainment. Know
                how and where to recruit musicians
                and entertainers, negotiate payment
                for services, keep them working to-
                gether as teams. Sell services for
                all kinds of occasions, keep business
                records, and make a profit.
```

Here's an example of another kind of Job Power Report. Hazel Brown was an orderly's assistant in a hospital. She also helped out at a kindergarten and in the high school office, and helped hospital nurses with their chores. Some of her attitudes at school were helpful in developing her Report:

```
JOB POWER REPORT OF..............HAZEL BROWN
                          114 23 Street
                 St. Jones, N.Y.  10016
                 Tel: HO5-2562
```

```
My Skills
Include:   On-time worker who is careful and
           neat, very good handwriting, good in
           typing, filing, bookkeeping and
           spelling; particularly good with
           children and in a health-care
           environment. Listen to and follow
           instructions well.
```

```
Proof:            No absences or lateness during three
                  years of high school; commended for
                  volunteer office work in high school;
                  sew my own clothes; invited to re-
                  turn after summer job at Bellevue
                  Hospital.  Good grades in all commer-
                  cial subjects.

Personal:         Passed Regents exams, age 17 1/2.
```

Another young woman of seventeen, **Betty Catin** is not clear about the environment in which she wants to work. While the contents of Hazel's Report would help Hazel get contacts in the health-care field, Betty's Report is not focused that way. Just the same, she does make it clear what some of her best skills are:

```
JOB POWER REPORT OF................ELIZABETH CATIN
                              142 East 42 Street
                              New York, N.Y.   10004
                              Tel: JE 4- 1415

Skills I
Can Offer:        Shorthand (90 wpm) and typing (65
                  wpm), pleasant telephone voice,
                  good in relationships with people,
                  good speller, a caring and respon-
                  sible person, memory.

Proof:            Earned Good Citizenship Award for
                  ability to get along well with
                  teachers and students; Leader of
                  Girl Scouts, and elected president
                  of camp; volunteer typist of forms
                  for people with housing problems;
                  high grades in typing, stenography,
                  spelling, English.

Personal:         Age 17, very good health.
```

You will notice that she did not include her height and weight (4'11", 118 lbs.). This is because some persons don't like short and chubby young women (or similar young men, for that matter), and you don't have to say anything against yourself in a Job Power Report. In any case, you will be hired because of your strengths, not because of what others may think is wrong with you. The Report should avoid stirring up unconscious prejudices that exist in each of us, while making your values, skills and talents very clear. It is quite different from Hank Wilson, 6'2". Height is helpful to a person with selling skill.

Now let's look at the Job Power Report of a person with no experience, someone who told his mother he'd like to be able to make some money during the summer, but didn't know what to ask for or where to go. His mother was a Haldane-trained job counselor, so she asked him to talk about things he felt he did well and enjoyed doing. He complained he felt like he was bragging, but the facts slowly came out. Then she helped him put them together, because he was only fourteen. And here's what his Report looked like:

```
JOB POWER REPORT OF................DAVID JAMES
                      2315 Winn Gills Drive
                      Cleveland, Ind.  41631
                      Tel: 266-5967
```

```
What I have
to offer:    You can tell what my skills are from
             these experiences.  They have re-
             quired responsibility, getting
             along with people, doing what is
             expected of me - and more, some prob-
             lem solving, some leadership, intel-
             ligence.

             I've been an honor roll student for
             2 years.  As Scout troop quarter-
             master I take care of all equipment
             and supplies; I am a Star Scout,
             and have been Patrol Leader, Senior
             Patrol Leader and Scribe.  I am on
```

the Human Relations Committee which
tries to solve school problems. I
volunteered for a daily summer re-
creational program for 80 grade
school children, leading them in
games, operating audiovisual equipment, etc. I was elected to the
Student Council last year. My daily
newspaper route covered three square
miles (6 months of it). And my
hobbies include reading, coin and
stamp collecting, camping and
canoeing, other outdoor activities.

I would like you to recommend me for
a summer job to someone who could
use several of my talents.

David thought it was too much to have all those little truths together. But the candy store owner he first showed it to said, "I didn't know all these things about you. You should show it to Mr. Sonninwell in the drug store. Lots of people go to him when they're looking to find someone to help out during the summer. Tell him I sent you."

David had met Mr. Sonninwell before, but using the candy store owner's name helped. However, the drug store man used the same words: "I didn't know these things about you, David. I'll keep you in mind if I hear of anything. But I think you should see Mr. Green over at the bank. I'll telephone and ask him to see you if you'll wait a moment." The banker said, after reading the Report, "You certainly should have a job this summer, and I'm going to call some of my friends about you. I'd like to make some copies of your Report to give to them."

David went home after that, with a very different sense of himself. He found that he was wanted for himself and his potential usefulness, and that his fear of talking to employers was largely gone. In his own way he used the procedures described in this book, going first to the candy store owner, giving him the Report and saying "Will you please read this and ask me some questions?" Those persons, and others he met in the same way, enabled him to find a summer job long before the end of June.

Janet Talley, a new college graduate of 20, was using an old-style resume. She had been looking for a special kind of work for six months, without success. Her resume gives a job objective in line with her college major of Economics, where she was in the top quarter of her class. Here's what her resume looked like after her name, address and telephone:

```
JOB WANTED
A tax or budget analysis, or a research job.

EDUCATION
B.A. Economics/Political Science, Jan.,1976, Uni-
versity of Kentucky.  Courses included statistics,
public finance, accounting, monetary policy, debate,
bureaucracy, organization behavior, group de-
cision making, legislative and executive branches.

Grade point average 3.45

EXTRACURRICULAR
National Women's honor society; president of cam-
pus Democratic Club; Girl Scout leader; on dorm
housing council.  National Organization of Women,
member.

EMPLOYMENT EXPERIENCE
University Housekeeping staff, two college years.
Hospital patients' secretary p/t, one year.
Receptionist at private clinic, p/t, one year.

HOBBIES
Mountain climbing, canoeing, travel, conversation,
consumer lobbying, investigating sex discrimination,
debating.

PERSONAL
Age 20, single.
```

Sure it looks good. But do you know what her skills are, or must you guess at them? And can you see that the job she asks for (tax or budget analysis, and research) requires her to be sitting at a desk working with figures and books all day, when her hobbies show she might prefer to be outdoors, traveling and talking. If there is no relationship between her employment experience (housekeeping, secretary, receptionist) and the kind of job she wants, perhaps she shouldn't mention it—unless she wants to be offered secretarial work, an unappealing prospect for a N.O.W. debater.

Janet's resume shows that the traditional way to go after a job can conceal your skills, making employers guess at them and therefore hesitate to consider you or offer you employment.

Job Application Form

The usual job application form is little different from the traditional resume. After asking for many personal facts which could be of no use unless you are employed (nine out of ten applicants are NOT employed), the usual form asks for your dates of work, a description of your job, name and address of employer, name of your supervisor, your rate of pay. What follows is this part of a modern job application form.

EMPLOYMENT RECORD List last five employers. List Last or Present Employer on top line.

EMPLOYER'S NAME AND ADDRESS	DATES FROM TO	JOB TITLE SUPERVISOR'S NAME	RATE OF PAY	REASON FOR LEAVING

Your rates of pay would be totally misleading if you hated the job or didn't do well in it, or if you took it just to make a few dollars for a while. Application forms also ask for permission to check up on your work with your former supervisors. But if you didn't get along with each other, which happens more often than is talked about, even if your work was good just contacting that person could lead to some doubt about you and therefore the loss of an opportunity both for you and for the organization. These negative situations don't happen all the time, but the traditional system and its forms enable it to happen much too often.

You should have ready, in your pocket or pocketbook, certain information you will need to put on application forms. Write the items carefully on a 3x5" card or in a notebook and carry it around with you wherever you go; it will save you lots of time and effort at remembering. This information is your Social Security number, your date and town of birth, where you now live and other places you have lived, full name of your father and your mother's maiden name, the schools you have attended—with dates, best subjects and grades. Also have the names of three people who could speak favorably of you as a person, but check with them first to make sure of what they might say and their willingness to have their names used.

Most of the time, if you use your Job Power Report as we suggest in this book, you will not have to complete those forms unless a job opening is available. However, you will always have to fill out a standard job application form before you are employed, unless you go to work for an organization with less than a dozen employees; even then some kind of job application is likely to be used. When you have the card in your pocket, you can pull it out and copy the dates and facts onto the form.

You will not necessarily have all the names, dates and places of employment on your Job Power Report, and certainly not the names and telephone numbers of persons who supervised you, so it is a good idea to have those names and telephone numbers on a small card in your pocket.

There are two times when completing job application forms could expedite your employment. The first is with government jobs. Most local, State and Federal agencies have a central bureau that distributes applications to all government agencies of the same type. If you complete and turn in your application it might reach a larger number of potential government employers than you can alone. The fastest-growing area of job opportunities is in state and local government agencies, and this growth is expected to continue for many years.

The second place that can distribute application forms to many potential employers is the large company personnel or employment office. For both places you will need to turn in one form and have another completed one to bring to interviews, so don't give up your own copy, except when an employer will immediately reproduce (Xerox) a copy for himself and return yours to you. In any case, you can't expect that circulating your application form is sure to get you a job offer. Until you have your job, you should keep on getting interviews by using the techniques given in Chapter Four.

How To Use Your Report

Your Job Power Report will help you in several ways. It will help you to have interviews without turndowns—which is the subject of the next chapter. It will help you avoid worry about forgetting important things to say at interviews. It will enable you to avoid filling out job application forms most of the time. It will help you know what to talk about at interviews. You can and should use it to influence an interviewer to ask the questions that help you put your best foot forward. It will reduce your fears and help you maintain self-confidence at interviews. It helps you practice what to say at job interviews. It also enables you to "be present" in several places at the same time, at least on paper, and makes it easy for you to reply to newspaper advertisements.

You will need about a hundred copies of your Report. Have someone type one (or two) copies for you. If you only have one, it can be photocopied or Xeroxed almost perfectly. Then paste the two copies on a full-size sheet of paper— 8 1/2 x 11"—and have an Instant Print or Quick Print firm make 50 copies, which you then cut in half so you have a hundred. You will find these printers in almost every city through the Yellow Pages of the telephone directory under the heading Duplicating Services. The cost for the printing should be less than $3.00. These small companies, your post office, or your library, can also make single copies of your Job Power Report at a cost of between 10c and 25c each.

Get practice in using your Job Power Report. Ask relatives, friends, classmates, neighbors to question you about what you say in it. Ask them to act like an employer or interviewer, while you act yourself looking for a job. If you are a Job Cooperative member, your practice opportunities are built into its operations. You'll find a section on practicing in Chapter 4, as well as a listing of questions employers could ask.

Here's one thing to practice with your Job Power Report: practice how you would act and what you would say when you go into an organization's employment office for a job. The first thing that happens, usually, is that you are given a job application form. You will need to feel comfortable about taking it, writing in your name, address, telephone and Social Security numbers, then attaching your Job Power Report to it, and returning it to the person at the desk. At that time, you would say something like this: "I'd really like an interview if you have a job opening up that would use the skills shown on this Report; I'll be glad to take the time to complete the rest of it if there are any openings. Will you please show this to the interviewer and let me know if he (she) will see me?"

The way your Report helps you to be several places at once is through the mail. You might see in the evening newspaper an ad for a job you would like to have, but you can't go after it because early the next morning you have another job interview. Well, you can put your Report in an envelope, address it to the place given in the ad, mail it at your late-pickup post office (there is at least one in every town), and it probably will be in the following morning's mail at the time you are having your interview elsewhere. You could use a pointed colored marker to write something like this on any Report you mail: "I can do that job you advertised. Please call me." And then sign your name.

Another way it helps your skills to be seen several places at once is through contacts who ask you for copies to show to other people they know (Chapter 4 tells you how to create contacts if you have none). And if you are in a Job Cooperative, your other group members will be using it to let their contacts know about your skills.

You should start using your Report this way. Make a list of four or five persons you respect, but who you believe would NOT have jobs for you—yes, would NOT have jobs for you, or even know of any. That's to make sure you will not be disappointed when they say they don't know of one. It will also help you to be comfortable when you say something like this, as you meet the first one: "I'd like to know if you think this Job Power Report will help me to get a job, or how I could improve it. I don't expect you to know of a job for me, but I'm looking." Then give your Report to the person and ask him to read it before asking you questions.

If you have done a thorough job of preparing your Report, the chances are he will not know all the facts you have put into it. So he's likely to be a little surprised, say so, and start asking you questions. This makes sure that he gets to know you better, and also remembers more clearly what you are looking for. Don't be surprised if he suggests you should put in things he knows about you, but which you carefully left out; but don't argue about why it should be in or out. ("Maybe I should put that in," is a safe comment to make.) Of course it is possible that he is right, although the chances are against that since you carefully selected—again and again—what you wanted to put in.

Then, when you've had your talk, if he doesn't ask for a couple of copies of your report, or doesn't give you another contact or two, ask him if he'd like one or two copies of your Report to show to people he knows who might have a job which would use your skills. Then, you take the same line with the others—who could include someone in a supermarket, a drugstore, a church, a community center, a service club, a scouting or similar organization, a police department, a social service worker. And if you see five persons, the chances are you will have four or five people using your Job Power Report to help you get a job. And the chances also are that they will give you contacts to several others who will bring closer the kind of job you want.

That Job Power Report, carefully prepared, is a powerful tool to help you get the kind of job you want much faster. Twice in 1975 and 1965, a report of the United States Department of Labor said that the approaches given in this book help more than twice as many young people get jobs in half the time compared with others who did not use these systems.

Summary

The Job Power Report samples given in this chapter show what information is left out, what is put in, and some ways they are used. These samples also indicate some practical solutions to the difficulties a young adult faces when looking for a job. Because of the common attitude among adults that young people have no experience and little to offer an employer, the Job Power Report helps the young job seeker to get these older persons to ask questions that prove their potential usefulness. It not only increases your employability but also the possibility that jobs will be created for you where none were thought to exist.

This chapter also reveals how to use the Report to answer newspaper ads, and how to initiate contacts with people who can help you find the job you are looking for.

Interviews, More Interviews

4

> *"We need jobs for self-esteem, self-confidence, character. Liberation struggles are built on sweat."*
> Jesse L. Jackson, director of People
> United to Save Humanity (PUSH)

THERE IS A PROVEN WAY to get job interviews without turndowns. It has been tested by high school and college students, and persons all the way up the line to government, university and corporate executives. It really works, works excellently. It has for more than 30 years. But it must be used carefully and thoroughly.

Because it's very different from the traditional way to get job interviews—it would have to be in order to assure that you get no turndowns—it must be explained so that it makes sense to you. First we'll give you a scenario, then an explanation, then the process details so you can do it yourself.

As with all systems in this book, if you work it out with a small group and practice the interview strategies you will find it easier to do consistently. And you will also find it easier to overcome mistakes you might make from time to time.

Here is the scenario, one application of the new job interview system:

Suppose a relative of yours has given your friend Mary an introduction to the manager of an organization where she would like to work. Mary has been told the supervisor probably does not have a job opening, but she has learned to apply all the systems given throughout these pages. After making an appointment she calls on the supervisor, and is shown into her office.

Mary:	Good morning Ms. Dixon. I appreciate your taking this time to see me at the suggestion of Mr. Brown.
Supervisor:	He said you would be a good person to talk to, Mary. Now how can I help you?
Mary:	First let me say I don't expect you to have a job for me, Ms. Dixon, although I am looking for one.
Supervisor:	That's fortunate. I'd hate to disappoint you. But what are you here for?
Mary:	I have several beginning talents, but because of my inexperience I don't know what kind of job would best use and and develop them. I'd like your advice about that. For instance, I can prove I'm very observant, I'm good at organizing things and papers, I can write clearly and effectively, and I get along well with people, among other things. This Job Power Report (hands executive her report) tells what my motivated skills are.
Supervisor:	(Look at report and quickly reads it) Well, that's quite a group of beginning skills. How can you prove them without work experience? I see you're about to graduate from commercial high school.
Mary:	Where would you like me to start, Ms. Dixon, with my ability to organize papers, my writing skills, or my relationships with people?
Supervisor:	Suppose you tell me about organizing papers.
Mary:	I think two examples will show that. First is that I'm known as 'lost and found' in my family—there are eight of us. Whenever someone loses anything and can't find it quickly, she turns to me. I ask a couple of questions, then I can usually go right to where it is. I've been finding things for the family for more than eight years, mainly because I have a sense of where everything is, so out-of-place items quickly show up. My second example is that I've been entrusted with taking care of the Principal's office files at high school and this is my second year of that. I set up the filing system after listening to her instructions, and I know where everything is. She depends on me to find and

	give her what she needs. Do you think these examples show beginning skill in organizing papers and things?
Supervisor:	Yes they do, Mary. And they also show people trust you and that you have a good memory. Can you give me good examples to prove your other beginning skills? I'm asking you this because I have another appointment soon. But I would like to spend some more time with you. I wish I did have a job for someone with your skills, because you're just the kind of person we'd like to employ.
Mary:	I can prove my other skills with different examples. And I would appreciate a little more time so I could get your advice. But since you do have to see someone soon, would you be able to suggest another executive I could see in the meantime who might be interested to know about my beginning skills, and also give me some advice on how to go about looking for a job? I wouldn't expect her to have a job for me, either.
Supervisor:	You've made a very good impression on me, Mary. I'd like to keep your Job Power Report, if you'll let me, and show it to some department heads in this organization.
Mary:	Yes of course, and thank you very much. (pauses carefully, to give executive time to respond more)
Supervisor:	(speaks carefully, slowly at first) Yes, I think I will give you an introduction. I'll call and make an appointment for you. But first let's make an appointment for ourselves when I'll be able to give you more time . . . . .

That's the scenario. Mary didn't ask for a job. She didn't fill out an application form. She didn't get turned down. She got Ms. Dixon interested in her skills and involved in her job-finding effort. She got referred to another supervisor and she also got a second appointment with Ms. Dixon. Between the appointments it is possible that Ms. Dixon would circulate her Job Power Report among her organization's department heads. And who knows what might happen between those two dates? One thing is sure: If Mary takes the same approach at her next interview—the one arranged by Ms. Dixon—she'll make it clear that she doesn't expect a job offer and again she won't be turned down.

This scenario makes it seem easier than it is. A lot of practice is needed in order to have an interview move this smoothly. It's a very different scenario from the traditional one, where you get turned down almost every time you ask for a job. Just imagine, briefly, what usually happens.

If you've ever spent more than four weeks searching for a job (thirty million men and women in this country did that in 1979), you were turned down many times. After you've been turned down a few times you're likely to experience an identity crisis and get somewhat depressed, maybe very depressed. You might even stop looking for a while, as most people do. The conventional procedure for getting interviews is usually a matter of filling out application forms; asking friends, relatives and neighbors to let you know where there might be job openings; knocking on employment or personnel office doors and waiting for interviews; sitting in waiting rooms while employment agency and public service placement specialists get around to telling you there are no openings—except occasionally the dead-end ones. Job hunting can be discouraging when you follow the beaten path, the traditional roads to job finding.

What a parent is likely to do to help a child get employment is to call a neighbor or friend and say, "Would you know of a job for my Mary (or my Jack)?" When asked what she can do, the parent might reply, "She doesn't have experience. What she needs is a start, an opportunity." Perhaps the parent would add, "She's a good student," or "a good athlete," or "keeps her room in order," or something else the parent especially likes.

It's a rare parent who will mention your skills, and be right about the ones you want to use in your job.

Most of the time the friend will respond, "Sure I'll be glad to help. If I hear of anything I'll let you know." But the silence is likely to be long, very long.

The parent wants to do what is best for you—in the

parent's opinion. But that might not be what you feel is best for you. A parent's judgment about what is best for you is likely to be based on the conditions that existed at the time she was your age. That's traditional, but it's not necessarily right.

Here are more key items in today's job market, which economists say are likely to prevail through the rest of the 1980's, with some ups and downs. (Just remember as you read these that this new system you are studying is not traditional, and increases job opportunities for young adults.) Most teen-age men and women entering the working world will change jobs 12 to 15 times during their working lives, and change careers three to five times. Another fact is revealed by a classified ad that appeared in *The New York Times* in the 1960's. It read, "DO YOU HATE PEOPLE? Here is an opportunity to turn down nine out of ten people you see. Job interviewer wanted. . . . ."

Another fact: a year-long study in a city of 400,000 people revealed that not one job in five is filled by the combination of personnel and employment departments, public and private employment agencies, newspaper ads, search firms. And just last year, a study in Illinois showed that about two-thirds of the jobs filled by public (free) employment services involved delivering telephone books, all of them dead end jobs.

These facts make it clear that the biggest part of the job market, 80 percent of it—where the best jobs are—is hidden. Our own and other studies show that these best job opportunities are reached through recommendations from one person to another. You'll soon see how to manufacture those contacts.

When you want to be recommended, you must be remembered. Mary, in the scenario at the start of this chapter, demonstrated what to do in order to be remembered and recommended. That's the "R & R Interview," one

71

which gets you remembered and recommended to someone else.

Think of what happens when you take the traditional approach and ask someone for a job, or if she knows where you can get one. In normal conditions asking for a job can be compared with asking for a special kind of help. To illustrate, look at an extreme situation: Let's say you cannot swim and you are near the end of a pier. You hear someone shouting for help. You look around but nobody is near and you cannot see a lifebelt. You see the person being washed out to sea, but you can do nothing. You will feel very badly about that situation, you'll wish you hadn't been walking along the pier, and you will try to forget all about that experience.

With job hunting, the person who is asked for help is generally in a similar situation—and you as a job seeker are likely to get one kind of literal response, and sense another reaction. The response from the friend or neighbor asked for job help is, "I'll do the best I can to help you, but you know the job market is tough. I'll let you know if I hear of anything." And the one you'll probably sense is, "I was hoping she wouldn't ask me that, because there isn't much I can do and I don't know of any job openings." That second reaction, the one you sense, is very dangerous.

No matter how consoling the words of your friend or neighbor, that reaction really says, "get off my back." The normal person doesn't like to be asked to give help unless it is immediately possible to provide that help. When you ask for job finding help you want it now. But almost always the person you ask is unable to provide the "lifebelt" of a job lead. So she feels badly about it.

You can expect most of the friends, neighbors and relatives you ask for job leads to feel badly about not being able to help you immediately. And also that the great majority of them will try to forget about *you*, since you caused that bad feeling. Tough, isn't it? But very real, and probably true to your experience and those of your friends.

Never Ask For A Job

Since most jobs—80 percent of them—are obtained through recommendations, it is unwise to do and say things that will cause you to be forgotten by friends, neighbors, and potential employers. The other jobs, the ordinary ones obtained through employment agencies, etc., are filled by means of job application forms. You can't easily turn off agency staff because they're experienced in turning people down hour after hour.

So your problem really is what to do about the friends, acquaintances, neighbors and others whose help you want, how to avoid making them feel bad and forget you.

Our advice, based on highly successful experience with tens of thousands of men and women of all ages is, "Never ask them for a job." Never ask for a job unless you have been told for certain that a job is open.

The advantages of not asking for a job include: You can't get turned down (you saw that in the scenario). You have not asked others to give help in a situation where they cannot immediately throw a lifeline. You have not caused them to feel badly about not being able to do something. And you have not started a process that will cause them to forget you and your interests.

On the positive side, if you speak in tune with reality and say at interviews, "I don't *expect* you to have a job or even to know of one," you decompress the tension that is always present at job interviews. You also enable the person to look you over, *and listen to you*, without feeling pressured either to hire you or to turn you down.

Employers like to "window shop" for employees. They

like to look people over without having any obligation to buy, or to hire. Further, employers almost hate turning people down, and nearly all of them have made serious mistakes when hiring employees. They don't like to be put under pressure to hire a person at an interview, or to feel they are being pressed by someone else's needs. That's a major reason why they have personnel and employment departments, and sometimes use employment agencies. These departments and organizations shield them from pressures, involvements, and the unpleasant task of turning people away. But executives haven't given away their hiring authority.

The R & R Interview

You can only be hired by a person who has the power to say "Yes." Executives and most supervisors have that power; personnel and employment managers have it only occasionally. Traditional job hunting methods have you register with the employment office, where the power to turn you down is strongest. The door there is always open, but you don't have to go through that door. You can get into the offices of supervisors and executives quite easily, especially if you have been recommended or given an introduction—the way Mary was at the end of Scenario No. 1.

The R&R Interview is designed to get you those recommendations and introductions. It requires you to get a number of persons involved in your job campaign. You need to get them to listen to your skills and talents, remember what you have to offer, and refer you to others, some of whom might employ you.

If you feel you don't know anyone who could refer you to possible employers, look at it this way: A grocery or drug store clerk could refer you to the assistant manager, and she could refer you to a salesman who could refer you to her

74

boss, who could refer you to her associates. Or, your friend's mother could refer you to her friend who happens to be a supervisor. A clergyman or a dentist could refer you to a parishioner or a patient. One of your teachers might refer you to another professional person who would pass you along to an executive or supervisor. Even a policeman you barely know has contacts that could lead to a job for you.

Here's how you get your interview contacts. First make a list of three or four starting contacts, ones you know you can reach without difficulty. Then make a second list of about ten you would like to reach, even if you know some of them only by their positions but not the people themselves.

At this point you have studied your achievements (Chapters One and Two) and written your Job Power Report (Chapter Three). You should have 100 copies of your Job Power Report.

If you have done those things, preferably with the help of a small group or Job Cooperative, you are ready for Scenario No. 2, which follows: Jim Jones is a young person and Barry Willis is his first contact.

Jim: Good morning Mr. Willis. Will you please look at this and ask me some questions? (hands him Job Power Report)

Willis: (Looks at JPR) You looking for a job?

Jim: I don't *expect* you to have one for me, Mr. Willis. But you could tell me if you think this Job Power Report will help me to find one.

Willis: It says here you can prove you have certain beginning skills. How can you prove you keep good records?

Jim: I'm business manager for the football team. I've arranged ten field trips this season, made arrangements for travel, meals, motel accommodations and other expenses for each of the team members, bought uniforms and equipment, kept records on all these items for each player, and the accountant checked everything as exactly right. In addition I maintain records on cards for each of the plays, and the players, and these are checked by each member of the team. I can give you some more examples of my record keeping if you want more proof, Mr. Willis.

Willis: I'd like to ask you about another beginning skill you say you have.

Let's pause to examine what's been happening: Jim has given Mr. Willis a very short statement of his beginning skills, and has asked his advice on whether his Report will help him to get a job. At the same time he took the pressure off Mr. Willis by saying he didn't *expect* a job offer. So Mr. Willis looked at the Job Power Report and started to ask questions. In other words, Mr. Willis became involved in Jim's job finding campaign, listened to him, became much more familiar with what he had to offer an employer.

Mr. Willis is virtually sure to remember some things about Jim. So the first "R," the Remember one, has been accomplished. Also, Jim didn't have to fill out an application form, and he wasn't turned down. Later in this interview, Jim handles the second "R," the Referral part. Here it is:

Willis: It seems like you can prove you have more than beginning skills there, Jim. So I'd say that this Job Power Report will help you get a job. I wish I knew someone who could use you. I'd be glad to recommend you myself.

Jim: Will you keep me in mind for the next three or four weeks, in case you do hear of a job opening for me?

Willis: I'll be glad to do that.

Jim: And I wonder if you know someone else, I wouldn't expect them to have a job for me, who might like to know about my beginning skills and keep me in mind in case she hears of a job opportunity for me?

Willis: Let me think. (pauses) I do know a couple of people who would like to talk to an ambitious young man like you, Jim. They wouldn't have jobs, but they know a lot of people. I'll write down their names and addresses, with their telephone numbers. Better call them first to make sure they're in, and use my name. (Writes down their names, etc., and hands to Jim)

Jim: Thank you, Mr. Willis. I'll let you know in a couple of weeks how I'm doing.

Willis: You do that. Good luck. Let me have a couple of your Job Power Reports for other friends of mine, and I'll call you as soon as I hear of a job for you.

Jim: Thank you again for your time and your introductions.

Let's examine what has happened in this part of the scenario. Mr. Willis gave Jim two interview contacts. He also agreed to keep Jim in his mind for several weeks, while job applicants usually are remembered for just a few moments after closing the door behind them. Willis also asked for extra copies of the Job Power Report to pass on to several of his friends.

When you use the R & R interview strategy it won't work this way all the time, but it will most of the time. Here's why:

1. It saves employers time when trying to find out what you can do, and lets them "window shop."
2. It saves contacts the embarrassment of turning you away when you ask for job help.
3. It shows you have taken the trouble to find out the skills you have to offer. This earns the respect of executive and professional persons and makes it unnecessary for them to guess at your skills.
4. It helps to maintain your morale during the job hunt, because you continue to get introductions and are meeting interested people.
5. It insures that you avoid job turndowns, and avoid filling out application forms unless jobs are available. This saves you a lot of time, stops you from becoming deeply depressed, supports your energy.

Practice What To Say

All interviews have their stresses, tensions, anxieties. The way to reduce these pressures substantially is by practicing what you might say at your interviews. Your skills and talents are the subject of the interview. You need to present them clearly, but you probably are inexperienced in doing that. Because you now have studied your Achievements, your Motivated skills and written your Job Power Report, you certainly know what you want to say to employers. Practice will help you to say the right things, and also reduce your tensions and anxieties at interviews.

In order to practice you need a person to take the part of an interviewer. Your best practice companion is an acquaintance, someone who has job-finding concerns like yours. Close friends or relatives will do if you have nobody else, but they are likely to be too easy with you. It is possible but difficult to practice by yourself, although this can be made easier when you use a tape recorder. From what we have said you can understand why we recommend as your best practice resource the Job Cooperative (Chapter 5). A group of about ten is ideal, but a smaller group of four or five is better than none.

Employers have their tensions, too; they don't know what to expect at a job interview. In their anxiety they could easily talk to fill-up time, and ask you questions about your home town, tell you about their own job hunting experience and early jobs, inquire about your birth, schooling, the careers of your parents. We call these "red herring trails" which take you away from the main subject of the skills you have to offer. Here is a practice-type scenario which shows how Wendy Watson handled a red herring trail question and brought the interview back on the track. Please assume that Mr. Hobbit and Wendy are already into the interview.

Hobbit: This Report gives a good presentation of your skills, Wendy, but you don't say where you were born.

Wendy: I left it out because I thought you'd want to concentrate on examining my skills and my potential, Mr. Hobbit. But I was born in Atlanta, Georgia.

Hobbit: That's a beautiful city, and growing fast into the most important center of the South. I spent a very happy four years there as manager of our Atlanta branch office. How long did you live there and how do you like it?

Wendy: Actually I lived there for the first twelve years of my life. I loved it. And while I was in school there I got my start as a leader, a problem solver with people, and as a writer. Of course I have developed since then, as you can see in my Job Power Report. Would you want to ask me about some more of the beginning skills mentioned in that Report?

Wendy had to practice a lot before she could be that smooth. But the scenario could just as easily have taken another turn, along these lines:

Hobbit: I see you're a freshman in Junior College. I'm always curious about the kind of work a person is looking for and the parents' occupations. There's a lot to heredity, you know. Please tell me what's your father's line of work?

Wendy: I may have inherited his skill with words, except I write more and talk less. He's a clergyman, and does a lot of counseling. Come to think of it, I'm very neat and a good organizer but his desk is always piled high with books and papers. He often asks me to help him organize it.

I'd much rather tell you about my skills, Mr. Hobbit. I can prove I have the beginning skills in my Job Power Report. It's a little embarrassing to talk about my parents. Could you ask me about the skills I listed? I would appreciate your advice on how to improve my Report or use it better.

Wendy has now talked for almost a minute; that's usually long enough to answer any question and then ask another question which gets the interview back on the track. But it takes practice to be brief in your answers, and also to make almost all of your statements into a comment on one or more of your skills.

Your purpose at an R & R interview—and they're all that kind unless you've been invited in to apply for a job—is to get the interviewer involved in helping you. This means first you must get him to read your Job Power Report and ask questions about your skills, and then get him to give you some advice on the kind of job your skills fit as well as how to go about getting such a job. You also want him to remember you and recommend you to others.

If you ask for a twenty-minute interview, you can't afford to have much time wasted talking about things other than your skills. It really takes practice, and that's where the Job Co-op is especially helpful, to work out how to take end runs around those questions that stop you from having good interviews. Here's another traditional block that is used, and a suggestion for an end run you can take.

You could be asked, "What were your best subjects, and where did you stand in your class?"

Your end run could be, "Some of my best subjects helped me to develop the skills shown in this Job Power Report (give it to him). Do you mind if I talk about them when I give you proof of my skills? (And then you wait for a minute or so while the interviewer reads your Report.)

You get the general idea of what you do at practice sessions? One person takes the part of the interviewer who does his best to guess at and do what he thinks an interviewer would say and do. The other is the job seeker. The job seeker should always act himself, and state in advance who he wants to be interviewed by (the President of General Motors, the Office Manager at the Supermarket, the Foreman in the machine shop, the Head Nurse at the hospital, the Office Supervisor at the bank, etc.). Then the interviewer should act that part, say the kinds of things and ask the questions he feels the person he is supposed to be would ask. You, as the job seeker, reply as you feel you would at a real interview with that person. It's almost like making up a real life play, and acting it out. You'll get the hang of it after you try it a few times; it will get easier.

Other members observe what happens. There should be a strict time limit of about fifteen minutes. After the interview ends the observers comment on what they saw and what was said, some might give suggestions for improving the practice interview, and the applicant and the interviewer then say how they feel about what they said and did. Then two other members practice an interview while the others observe. Comments, feelings and exchanges of ideas go on as before. Each time there is a practice session each member learns something new. Part of the time he gets into how the employer feels and acts, at other times he feels with a particular situation presented by the applicant, at other times he gets feelings about what he himself might do and say.

An interview is a very complex situation, where neither party knows for sure what will be said or happen next. If you have a good idea of what you want to say about yourself, if you practice saying it and getting around possible obstacles raised by the interviewer, you are more likely to feel only reasonably anxious at your interviews instead of very anxious.

You should do most of your practicing with questions that are most likely to be asked. You'll find many of these in the following pages. You will also find there some questions you should ask when you are offered a job.

You will very likely be asked several of these questions at both R & R and at job interviews. You should get practice in answering them with a friend or with your Job Cooperative; sometimes, when answers could be dangerous (*), you will need to practice how to turn them around. This list is not in order of importance, and other questions could be asked on occasion.

1. Why do you want to work here?
2. How did you happen to come to us?
*3. Why did you leave your last job? (Be sure you say nothing against any employer. If you had a personal difference, you could say "We agreed to disagree." If you were fired for incompetence, say, "We agreed I should do some other kind of work, just like I indicate in my Job Power Report." Whatever you do say, make it truthful, and as much in your favor as possible. Wherever you can, turn it back to your skills and Report.)
4. How long have you been out of work?
5. How did you like working with your former employer?
*6. Tell me about yourself? (Make sure you refer the interviewer to your Job Power Report. You could say, "I'd like to tell you about my dependable skills which have begun to develop. Will you please take a minute to read them in my Job Power Report?" Then, when he looks up, say "Which one would you like me to start with?" This question is expected to get you confused, and say something like, "I was born at an early age.")
7. What did you like least in your last job?
8. Tell me about the hardest job you ever did?
9. What do you do in your spare time? Last week?
10. Tell me about your health?
*11. Suppose you get hired. What do you see as your future here? (If you expect to stay, talk about opportunity to develop your skills, learn how to be more useful, do things that will earn promotions, make friends with some other employees.)

*12. What else do you think I should know about you? (Never say anything against yourself. You could say, "because I travel a long way, and traffic conditions sometimes get very tough, I might get in late. But I put in extra time when it's needed to finish my work.")

*13. What are some of your weaknesses? (Again, turn this around. If you are going for a writing job, you might say, "I'm really not mechanical, and if I got a flat I might not be able to change tires. But that won't affect my writing work." What this ploy does is get things back to where both you and the employer get the benefits—using your best skills.)

14. How much money do you expect?

And Your Questions

Now there are some questions you should ask at interviews where you are being considered for a job. You do want to have a description of your duties and responsibilities, because that lets you know when you're doing what's expected. And it also enables you to know, when you are doing things right, that you can ask for more responsibilities.

You should also get the name of the department you'll work in, the name of your immediate supervisor and the name of the department head; and write them down so you won't forget. The regular working hours must be known.

It is also helpful to inquire about what kind of training you will be given. And you will want to know what your starting salary is.

During the ten-to-thirty interviews you could have before getting the job you want you will notice a couple more questions that you seem to attract. Be sure to practice answers to them as soon as possible.

In most medium-size companies, and all larger ones, there is a manual for employees which tells about Social Security, Federal Income Tax and other payroll deductions, as well as pension plans and the general rules and regulations of the organization. It often is called an *Employee Handbook*, and you should ask for it. You should also ask for something that describes the activities of the organization or company, and become familiar with what generally goes on and the purposes of your organization and your department. This knowledge will be very useful when the time comes for you to seek a promotion—perhaps into another department. Most new jobs are in small companies. That means you will need many interviews.

Attitudes, Appearance

There will come a time when you are required to have an R & R interview with a personnel manager. Before the interview you will be asked to complete a job application form. We suggest you handle the situation as we did before, in this way:

Put your name, address and telephone number on the form, attach a copy of your Job Power Report (with a paperclip or pin), and turn it back in with the statement, "If you have a job that will use the skills shown on my Job Power Report, I'll be glad to fill in the rest of the form." Say that quietly and with confidence, and your interview will be better than if you simply do as you're told and complete the form before the interview. You will maintain your self respect and probably gain more attention from the personnel officer.

Remember that you must feel comfortable in your dress and in your speech at interviews. What you look and sound like can help you to get the job you want. You do need to dress appropriately, just as you would if you were a bridesmaid at a wedding. You might fix your eyes for that, but the same style of eye makeup would not necessarily be appropriate for a job interview. It might be if you were after a cosmetics salesperson job, but not if you wanted a steel factory job. In a department store job you might be able to wear sandals. But in a factory where there are heavy materials moving around on cranes, conveyors and fork trucks, you must wear safety shoes, so for a job in that kind of factory, go for an interview with regular shoes on (the company usually provides safety shoes).

Different kinds of jobs have different safety regulations which influence the kinds of dress that are appropriate. In a bank job, for instance, very loose hair could prevent you from quickly seeing a holdup or preventing an accident, and stylish blue jeans could suggest to an employer that your integrity might be overstrained by your poverty. You don't have to go completely square or conservative in order to have good job interviews, but you do need to be appropriately dressed. You can find out what appropriate dress is by asking people, especially those who have professional or supervisory positions. You need not take their exact word for what is appropriate, but you should consider their suggestions. It is in this area, again, that the small group or Job Cooperative can be especially helpful. There, people your own age can help you to make up your mind on what is appropriate.

A couple of things are standard. Bathe or shower every day you have interviews. Your clothes should be reasonably neat and clean. If you use perfume or after-shave, the scent should not be conspicuous. As a general rule, it is better to wear shoes than sandals, and your dress, pants or suit should be more on the conservative than on the casual style. All makeup and hair styling should be in harmony with your clothes.

Because there always is stress at interviews, you may be so nervous that you speak too fast, stutter, or are otherwise not clear in what you say. Practice what you want to say, and you will find it easier to speak more clearly. One of the special advantages of the R & R interview strategy is that by giving the contact your Job Power Report, and asking him or her to question you about it, you can be reasonably well prepared in your answers. The facts you need for your answers were developed when you worked on identifying your skills pattern (Chapter 2), and while working out your Job Power Report. If you are working with a group you can take turns at practicing what you will say when you are asked questions about your background.

Keep in mind that every contact you make, every interview you have, should be considered as an R & R interview unless and until it is a job interview—where you have been told there is an opening for your skills.

Money Matters

You are being interviewed for an available job when an interviewer says something like, "I have a job that could use your skills," or "I'd like to get you into our beginners' training program." Your concern then is not how to be remembered and referred, but how to get a firm job offer with a starting date and rate of pay.

So you change tactics, and you start asking the questions to get job facts. First of all you say something like this: "I'd like to work in your organization. I think there will be opportunity to develop my skills, and get ahead. Can you tell me just what this job requires?"

Then you listen carefully, and you should make some notes (in a notebook that should be with you at all kinds of interviews). Remember that you can't write and listen completely at the same time, so check the correctness of your notes with your interviewer. Chapter 6 will tell you how to handle the interview where you know there's a job, and the various situations and choices it presents.

On the matter of money, there is something special we have to suggest.

First the bad news! If the employer suggests the minimum wage as your starting rate of pay, and especially if you feel you are worth more than that, don't turn down the job. We advise that you never turn down a job when it is first offered to you, even if it's shoveling manure in a pig pen (one of your authors has done just that as part of a job). Each job offer, and you will receive many during your working life, is a compliment that says someone thinks well of you or cares for you. An abrupt turndown ("I don't want that kind of work") is like spitting in the wind.

Our experience shows that every kind of job offer can be turned into something better, and every starting pay can be raised. Sometimes you cannot make the change happen immediately, but you can feel sure that every sincere job offer leads to something better—even if you eventually must turn down the job offer.

You are different from most beginners. Hardly any of the others have studied themselves the way you have. They have not given proof of their skills; the employer has guessed at their skills and hopes he is somewhere close to right. With you, he knows your skills and there is no guessing. That makes you worth more than most of the other beginners.

So the good news is that you should ask for higher pay, regardless of what you are offered. You may not get it at once, but you might if you go about it in the right way.

You could say—if you have enough courage—something like this: "Ms. Dixon, you say I would start at the regular beginner's rate of pay. But because I have *proved* what my skills are, and you probably have had to guess at the skills of most other beginners, don't you think it would be fair to start me at a slightly higher pay level?"

Even if it's only 10c an hour higher, that's about $4 a week more. Maybe they'll give it to you, maybe they won't give it. Unless you do it in an aggressive way, there's nothing lost by trying; and if it's 25c an hour more, that comes out to $10 a week. What's likely to happen, at worst, is that your Ms. Dixon will say, "We have a policy that starts all beginners at the same rate, and I'm afraid we can't break that rule just for you."

If that happens you do have another ploy available. You can respond, "I wouldn't want you to change the policy, Ms. Dixon. But I think my supervisor will find that my work improves very quickly. If he does find out that I learn quickly and am highly productive, would I be considered for a raise in a month or two?" An approach like that should really bring you a positive response.

Now when it comes to some activity in the job that you don't like, you can always ask for more of some parts of it that you do like and less of what you don't want. Unless you ask, you don't know what's possible. But don't think that because you ask you will get what you want. Sometimes, fairly often, an unpleasant task is a necessary part of a very good job—much like chopping onions and a good dinner. One thing is certain: most employers will change elements of a job in order to get an employee who will do dependable work.

When you have the pay question settled, you must be clear about when you get started. Suppose you are offered the job on Tuesday, and you are asked to start the following Monday, there's nothing to prevent you from asking if it is possible for you to start the next day, Wednesday. It could mean three extra days of pay in your pocket, and those extra days of service for the organization. If you want to start earlier, or later within reason, if you ask you can probably have your way.

Employment is a kind of contract. You agree to join a

small or large organization and handle certain responsibilities in return for a sum of money you both have agreed on.
If you do better than the organization expected, you are
likely to get a pay increase, sometimes together with a
higher-level job. If you don't do as well as was expected of
you, your pay and job can be terminated. If you do better,
but fail to get a pay increase, you are free either to
complain and negotiate for what you feel you deserve, or
you can look for another job which does reward you in a
more satisfying way.

As a young adult entering the job market you are
moving into a life-zone that constantly hammers at your
identity. Some experts say you can expect to be job hunting
again within a year, and again about each 18 months for
another 20 years. Each time that happens your identity is
threatened. But you have already developed a dependable
means for maintaining the integrity of who you are. Knowledge of your skills pattern, and your motivated skills stated
in your Job Power Report, will be with you for the rest of
your life. You will be able to use those skills, honed by
experience, training and education, to meet the demands of
changing job titles and changing economic needs. Your dependable skills and talents, your motivated skills, are
strong threads of continuity that run through the changes
that are coming at an ever faster pace.

You can use your motivated skills knowledge either to
get ahead and change your job with a single employer, a
process that can be repeated many times, or you can use it
to change jobs and careers as you move from one employer
to another. If you are to stay with one employer for any
length of time you will need to establish good relationships
with your co-workers and your supervisors. You will also
need to bring your Job Power Report up to date each year,
by keeping monthly or quarterly records of your on-the-job
and other achievements. What you find out about your

growing skills will need to be communicated to your supervisor, tactfully. Then she will be able to check your facts, and occasionally change your job and your financial rewards for doing work of greater value to the organization.

Summary

The interview without turndowns is the R & R interview. It helps you to be remembered and get referred, it enables you to create contacts of many kinds, and it gets you around obstacles of job application forms and personnel departments. After you have identified your dependable pattern of skills or talents (Chapters 1 and 2), and after you write your Job Power Report (Chapter 3), you have a handle on how to prove and improve your motivated skills, how to combine them in different ways to meet the requirements of changing job conditions. In this chapter, you learned how to talk about this expanded self-knowledge at an interview that leads to the creation of more contacts and interviews— soon leading to job offers. You also learned about practicing what to say at these interviews and how to ask for better starting pay and a pay raise.

Job
Cooperative

5

"Every event has an undiscovered meaning, every experience is directed towards some new and greater unfoldment of potentials hidden deep within oneself."
Marcus Bach

FIVE MAJOR FEARS hit new job seekers. Fear of not getting a job quickly. Fear of getting the wrong one. Fear of dependency on relatives for job finding. Fear of what to say at interviews. Fear of ignorance, neither knowing what kind of job to look for nor where there might be job openings. To these could be added, fear of being unemployed for a long time and fear of running out of money so that you are not truly independent.

The Job Co-op enables you to cope with these fears. It enables you to create job contacts wherever you want them—so you are much less dependent on relatives. It gives you training in job interview strategies, help in knowing your best skills and how to present them in a Job Power Report. It helps you to know what kind of job to look for, and where. It enables you to know in advance the kinds of opportunities that exist in a variety of fields of work.

Research studies in 1965 and 1973—one in urban New Jersey, the other in a California rural area—have proven that group and peer counseling cuts job finding time by

more than half for the great majority of participants.*
When you are with a group you have a better chance to
check with others on how to develop your Job Power
Report, better opportunity to practice the R&R Interview,
more likelihood that you will spot contacts and job openings for each other, and be more available to help each
other surmount depression when progress seems to be slow
or even negative. You can also help each other to correct
mistakes—you'll find that the more progress you make the
more opportunity there is to make some mistakes.

In addition to cutting job-finding time by more than
50 percent, which effectively deals with the fear of running
out of money, the Job Co-op helps you to overcome job
finding problems that occur from time to time; it provides
boosts to your morale—much needed when job interviews
come slowly; it helps to expand your potential as a person;
and it gives you guidelines for getting promotions, pay increases and changing jobs again when the need may arise.

The companionship in trial, and believe us job hunting
is a trial of your identity, plus the excitement of knowing
that what you say may help another member get that
wanted job—all these and more are value components of
the Co-op which are usually missing when you work on the
job hunt by yourself. Of course you CAN do it on your own;
no question on that. But the Job Cooperative gives an
added dimension, to your victories and growth.

A Job Co-op is ideally a group of ten young adults, associated with high school, a local service club, a Junior
College, an area block or blocks. It can be any number of
multiples of eight-to-ten persons; it should not be less than

---

* Florence Bustamante, on a Haldane-type program, in *MAN-
  POWER*, U.S. Department of Labor, Dec. 1965.
  Azrin, Flores and Kaplan—a job club program with mentally
  retarded, in *Behavioral Research & Therapy,* Vol. 13, 1975.

four. Each member should be concerned with finding a job quickly, and with helping each other to do that. Each member should be looking for work in a different field.

In summary, here is what happens: Each member completes the self-study program detailed in Chapters One and Two, and helps the others to identify their skills, talents, strengths. Then they check with each other on the Reality Test details which prove those strengths or motivated skills. Next they help each other to develop their Job Power Reports and in the practice which enables them to be effective when using those reports. After that they plan a strategy to study how people become successful, how to be effective at interviews, how to get job leads for each other and themselves—even where it seems that there are none. And, finally, they help each other overcome or cope with difficulties and depression when things progress slowly.

Here is what happened at one Job Cooperative. Bill was skeptical about trading his time for what he felt was a rap session about jobs. He didn't see much benefit in it for himself, but was willing to look in for a half-hour to see what goes on. He joined four participants, who were expecting others.

Bill: What goes with this Job Co-op thing?

Mary: We're practicing job interviews right now, but come on in, Bill.

Bill: I'm not staying, just curious on what you do. How can talking about jobs help me get one? Go on, show me.

John: We *can* show you, Bill. And it won't take long for you to see. We had to do a lot of things before being able to do what we'll show you. What we'll demonstrate is just one part—how to use a Job Power Report to get someone to interview you and not turn you down.

Bill: I've had a lot of interviews, and got turned down every time. It's not real, man. I'm splitting. I got no time for this crap!

Jane: Billy, don't you go running off without listening. All you do is shoot your mouth off, and run. How you going to find out what we do if you don't stay. We're with you about wasting time. And we're not wasting time being in this Job Co-op. That's true, isn't it?

Mary/John/Alex:

Jane's right, Bill.

Alex: Listen, and make up your mind when you know what we're about.

Bill: Okay. Do your stuff. Do your stuff!

Mary: You've had a lot of interviews, Bill. Then you know what questions interviewers ask. You take the part of a boss, and interviewer. And I'll be interviewed by you. Okay?

Bill: Okay, I'll give you a hard time.

Mary: I just would like you to look at this and ask me some questions, Mr. Bill. (gives him Job Power Report)

Bill: We're not hiring now.

Mary: I don't expect you to have a job for me, but I would like ten minutes of advice on if you think my Job Power Report will help me to get a job. Will you take a minute to read it, then ask me some questions, please?

Bill: (reads it) I told you we got no jobs.

Mary: And I told you I don't expect you to have a job. But you could tell me if you think my Report could help me, or not.

Bill: You're not out of high school yet, you never worked. So how can you say you can prove you're good in writing, research, finishing jobs you are given.

Mary: Those are some of my beginning skills, Mr. Bill. I've been reporter and editor of my school paper for two years, and one article I researched was picked up and printed by the Washington Post. My teacher says I'm an "A" student because I finish every job I take on. I've turned in every class assignment on time for at least two years. Most of them required some library or field research. Do these experiences prove I have some skills in writing, research, and finishing jobs, Mr. Bill?

Bill: You said that real good, Mary. Sure it proves you have those skills. But how come you didn't lose your cool when I was so rough with you? You really got me interested in what you were saying.

Mary: Mr. Bill, do you think this Job Power Report will help me get a job?

Bill: Sure it will, if you can do what you did with me when you're at an interview. But then, everybody says they don't have any jobs. How do you get around that?

John: You can't get everything in five minutes, Bill. She got you in-

94

terested in her skills, even though you were very rough with her. There's a lot more to it. You tried to throw her out of your office, but she stayed right in there and got you interested. Isn't that enough to show we're not wasting our time? You want to join our Co-op?

Bill: Once she said she didn't expect me to have a job for her, even after I told her twice I had no jobs, I started to look at her as an unusual person.

Mary: That's it! Employers think that every kid coming to them is trying to get on a payroll, that all kids are the same. Only what I did made you think I must be different. So you were willing to give me extra attention. Well, that's part of the game of getting a job, getting yourself seen as different and special. But that's only one of the things we learn and practice in this Job Co-op.*

Bill: Okay, okay! I'm joining. Maybe there's more to this Job Cooperative than I thought.

Alex: It's like running a race, or playing football. It takes a lot of practice to learn how to say what Mary did, to keep her cool when she was faced with an employer trying to get rid of her. And she had to do a lot of studying of herself before she knew what she could say about her skills. But we all helped her, and she helped us, too.

Jane: What we're doing next is about getting interviews, and researching how people get started in the kinds of jobs we want.

Let's examine two very different situations that show the type of help a Job Co-op can provide. One involves a high school dropout of 17, who often was in trouble with the police. The other involves a bright 18 year-old, the son of upper-middle-class parents who each have two or more college degrees. The dropout speaks poorly, a listener can hardly understand him. He is small, his back is arched. He says he wants to be an electrical worker on houses. We'll call him Joe.

Joe was in an experimental Job Co-op six years ago. The Job Power Report he wrote in semi-legible writing read like this:

---

* Job Cooperative activities are more effective when conducted with the assistance of a trained facilitator, teacher, or businessperson.

I work good installing all kinds of electric wiring
in house construction. Any kind of electric installing I can do. When you ask me about it I don't
talk too good, but I can show you how I do it.

In our Job Co-op he was not able to talk about his skills; he just mumbled "I know it" when asked questions about various kinds of electrical wiring work. Another member of the group, a young woman, asked him to show us how he'd go about installing some new wiring. He instantly became alive, went to the wall, and showed what he would do while he talked about how he would cut the wall, the kinds of wiring, pipe and tools he would use to make that installation. It was convincingly clear that he knew what he was doing and talking about.

But because his writing, his speech and his appearance were not good he had been unable to get a job for many months. He really was scared at job interviews. Others in the Co-op helped him practice giving his Job Power Report to a construction foreman, asking him to read it, then responding to his questions along these lines: "Mister, I don't expect you to have no job for me. I just know how to install electric wiring so it meets the code. I don't speak good. I don't write good. I can show you how I go about installing any kind of wiring. I want to be an electrician helper, and later to be an electrician when I get experience enough. Will you test me, and then advise me how I could get some more work experience?"

When he could see how the others were helping him, he gave them some of his street wisdom and was very helpful. And with their help Joe had a job in two weeks, a job he found on his own.

The other young man, Walter, had been in business for himself since age fourteen, collecting and selling stamps. He kept detailed records of his stamps, kept the household records, and later—while still in high school—kept financial records for small businesses under the supervision of an accountant. Because he was legally too young to be involved in accounting, he kept these activities to himself until high school peers in a Job Co-op gave him freedom to talk about his achievements and write his skills in a Job Power Report—like this:

I am accurate and dependable in keeping detailed

financial records, including double-entry book-

keeping, monthly and quarterly statements and yearly

balance sheets. I have worked with an accountant

for over three years, and he has often audited my

work without finding errors. I work fast and learn

quickly. I know something about keeping records

for tax forms. And I get along with people

very well.

Walter went to college, became the first freshman to audit the scholarship endowment fund, was treasurer of the bookshop, and in similar ways got jobs and gained a reputation for dependability in financial matters. He sent his Job Power Report to alumni near his home, and they helped him get a summer job that used his skills.

The interesting thing about these two very different people is that Walter, when joining the Co-op, was confused about what kind of work he wanted—partly because he believed he could do many things, and partly because he had feelings of guilt about doing work which he couldn't legally do because of his age. On the other hand, Joe was confused because he couldn't get people to believe he knew what he did and was a valuable worker. Walter had opportunity in college, and in his part-time jobs, to broaden the application of his skills, and also to strengthen them—but he was aware of what skills he was strengthening because his best skills were clarified while in the Job Cooperative.

Working World Research

Let's look at the way members of the Job Co-op explore the different fields of work. At this point each member of the Co-op has gone through the stages leading to completion of the Job Power Report, and each has about a hundred clear copies of it.

Each member gives the others one copy of his or her Job Power Report. Each binds them into a file folder, in alphabetical order by name, with your own on top inside your file. Reading the reports will show that you are each looking for jobs in different areas of work. Let's say one person is in the field of figures, and others are in such areas as personnel, sales, electronics, practical nursing, hospital orderly, automobile repair, typing, butchering and receptionist-type work.

You now are ready to do some research on how people start and become successful in these different work areas, and also to explore a new way to create job contacts and leads—for yourself and your Co-op members.

You will need to be acquainted with the skills and general aims of other members of your team, and then decide among you which work area to research—because you must *not* research the area of your own interest. However, the organization to be researched should be selected by the person with the interest in that area of work. For instance, if John wants to be in the personnel field, and Mary wants to be in the auto mechanic area, John says he'd like to know how the personnel manager of Hotspur (the local big private employer) made it into that job, and Mary says she wants to know how the maintenance boss of the Chevrolet dealership got to his position. The other eight also select where they would want jobs researched.

Then you have to do that research in a special way which makes sure that you'll get the information you want—which is how a person gets started in your area of work interest, and how he gets ahead. The basic steps you take are these:

1. Get the name of the person in that position, telephone and arrange an appointment.
2. Keep the appointment, interview him or her to get the information you want.
3. At the same time, stir up interest in the Job Cooperative and the members of your group.
4. Report back to the group, first the information you went for, and then additional information on what else happened at the interview.

You have two purposes at that interview. One is to learn about the world of work through the person you interview. The second is to *help that person* become interested in the Job Cooperative idea.

Let's assume you are students at the John Xavier High School. To get the name of the person in that job, the person you want to see, call the main telephone number of the organization and ask the operator for his name, proper title, and the correct spelling of both. It could go something like this, if we assume that Mary's going to interview the Personnel Manager, and John's to interview the Chevy maintenance boss. Mary calls the number and says, "Could you give me the full name of your Personnel Manager please? I'm a member of the John Xavier High School Job Cooperative, and I need to know his name."

The chances are that you'll get it, in which case you ask (and write it down) "How does he spell that?" Or, you'll be referred to his secretary. If the second thing happens, be sure to get her name, wait while you are being transferred, and then speak along these lines:

"Miss Jones, I'm Mary Brown. I'm a member of the John Xavier High School Job Cooperative. We're researching the working world, and I have to interview your Personnel Manager to find out how he became successful and how he got started. I must report that back to our Job Co-op. Would you please tell me his full name, and spell it out for me, and also arrange a half-hour appointment for me with him."

Now there is a chance that you'll be put right through to the person, and then you have to say something like Mary said to his secretary—except that now you'll be asking him directly for the appointment.

You won't have to worry about what to say on the telephone if you write it out clearly so you can read it when you're on the phone. Just be sure to mention the Job Cooperative, your school or sponsoring organization, and that you want to be able to report back to the Co-op how that Personnel Manager became successful and got started.

When you go to the appointment, take along your file of Job Power Reports and a large notebook for writing down what the Manager, Maintenance Boss or other executive says. You won't have to write down everything, but you will have to make some notes.

Here is what happens at a good Working World research interview. You arrive at the appointed time. You may have to wait a few minutes but usually you'll get in promptly. The person asks what you want to know, and you say—with a smile if you can manage it—"The members of my John Xavier High School Job Co-op want to know how a person in your position becomes successful, and how you got started. We're exploring the working world and its beginning opportunities." Then you listen carefully and make some notes on what is said.

If you are asked questions about yourself, give your file of Job Power Reports to the person and say, "The top one tells you about me" or, "The top one's mine."

If the person asks about the Job Co-op, say something like this: "The purpose of the Job Co-op is to help each member become aware of his or her best skills and talents, develop honest proof of them, summarize them in a Job Power Report, practice how to talk about them at interviews, research the working world and help each other to know what it is, then help each other to get job contacts and land a job. Right now, with you, my task is to research the working world." You can write down and read a statement about what the Job Cooperative is, but you should *not* give what you have written to the person to read for himself.

If the person asks you about others in the Co-op, refer him to the other Job Power Reports in your file, saying that they're in alphabetical order. The chances are that he'll want to look at several Reports, and may even ask permission to make copies of them. When or if that happens, let the copies be made. But be sure you get to the point of your interview—how did he become successful, and how did he get started.

And at the end of the interview, do ask if he or she might be interested in meeting one or more of the Co-op members, in which case you'll be glad to have that person telephone. If you don't ask, you're not likely to receive. There's a lot to be gained by asking, and nothing to be lost.

KEEP IN MIND THAT YOU ARE INTERVIEWING THE EXECUTIVE OR BOSS FOR THE JOB CO-OP. YOUR BUSINESS IS TO GET THAT INTERVIEW, and report back to the Co-op members. If you gain something on the side, such as contacts for other Co-op members or for yourself, that's a bonus and for free. Accept graciously what is offered—but you MUST NOT accept a job offer while you are on your Working World research. If you should be offered another interview, and then a job, be careful. It doesn't happen often, but if it does you should say something like this: "One of the rules of this Working World research is that we cannot accept a job offer until after we report back to the Co-op. We'll be meeting next week to give our reports to each other, and (if you want the job) I'll be glad to start working right after that. Is that OK with you?

But if you don't want the job, you may need to say something like this: "Our rules for this Working World research require me to report your job offer to the Co-op. Is it OK with you if I call you right after our report meeting next week? Then I'll be free to talk about working with your fine organization."

A lot of employers want to hire—even create jobs for—young men and women who really have studied their lifetime or motivated skills and talents. It is no harder to go after the job that will bring you fulfillment than it is to go after one that brings you only a paycheck. As a matter of fact, the one which brings you fulfillment and growth opportunities is also likely to bring you a fatter paycheck. The majority of our clients, over a thirty-year period, have told us that. And tests of programs using the job finding techniques given in this book demonstrate that pay differences at the start will usually be ten percent higher.

Report what happened at the interview to your next Job Co-op meeting. Members of the Co-op should be allowed just one week for their interviews with employers. If you have a group of ten, perhaps one or two will have run into a problem such as sickness of the Co-op member or the employer, or a sudden demand that takes the employer out of town. Perhaps someone else will contact an employer and find him unwilling to be interviewed; it's not very likely, but it does sometimes happen. In a case like that, ask him to suggest the name of someone in another organization, a person who has the same type of position, whom you might call. Tell him that you won't use his name, but that you need to get an interview so you require his help. With that very reasonable approach, the chances are that you'll be able to get a substitute interview within the week.

At your Working World report meeting of the Job Co-op, listen to all the interview reports. Just as you will have some unexpected experiences to report, so will the others. Perhaps one of them will have been asked, on the basis of giving his or her Job Power Reports file to the employer, to suggest that you call for a job interview. You will also hear about different ways many people got started in their jobs, and how they moved ahead. You won't want to copy any of those ways because you are a different person, but knowing about their ways will help you to make choices of your own.

Equally important will be the understanding you develop of how to get in to see employers, and some of the best ways to respond to their questions without becoming too anxious. Some of you will have job leads, most of you will have helped open doors for the others to make contacts with possible employers in the organizations. And all of you will have built respect in those organizations for young men and women who take the trouble to study their motivated skills through the Job Cooperative. Nearly all of those employers will talk to their friends about your interview and the Job Co-op, and some of their friends are certain to want to meet one or more of the Co-op members.

All this work makes sense, doesn't it? And it really doesn't take very much time.

The Working World research report meeting should last at least two hours, because in addition to listening to each other you will have lots of names and stories to exchange. After that, you should begin arranging your interviews—as described in Chapter Four. Give yourselves enough time to have about four R&R interviews—three days if you are a full-time job seeker—then meet again to discuss what happened at those interviews.

You need to meet twice a week, or at least once a week, while you are seriously job hunting. At those follow-through meetings you should take turns telling about your experiences at interviews. Do not give your own contacts to the other members, but you should pass along contacts that don't interest you. When you are doing R&R interviews you will find that employers and friends often ask if you know someone with skills other than your own. They also occasionally reveal knowledge of other kinds of jobs that are open, and people who are looking for certain kinds of skills. Well, the Co-op is the place to share the information you don't want for yourself.

But there's another special benefit to frequent follow-through meetings. Your fellow members can help you to overcome problems and cope with disappointments, and you can help others in the same way. You see, every interview, even the friendliest one, contains some stress. And where there is stress you have the possibility of forgetfulness, of saying the wrong things, of overlooking the procedures you have trained yourself to use. When you talk about them at the Job Co-op, others will be able to notice what happened and suggest ideas that will help you to recover lost ground, or otherwise cope with the situation.

For example, one young woman reported accepting a job, but she had forgotten to ask about the starting pay. After a lot of laughter, some of it embarrassed, the collective wisdom was that she should immediately go to the store where she was due to start the next day and discuss pay along these lines: "In my excitement about starting this job, which I just love, we didn't get into the matter of pay. I take it that because I have proven skills you do not consider me a beginner, and so my pay will be above the usual starting one. Can you tell me what it will be?" The employer was kind and smiling as she said it would be 25 cents an hour ($10.00 per week) above the regular starting pay rate. They smiled at each other, the Co-op member said, "See you tomorrow morning," and that was that. Nobody will ever know if she would have been given the regular beginners pay rate, but we do know she is getting more than other starters would.

Now let's go more deeply into the ways that Co-op membership can help you with finding your best lifetime skills, your *motivated skills,* aid you in Reality Testing them, enable you to practice interview strategies, and counsel you on your Job Power Report.

When you first started remembering and studying your achievements, in Chapter One, we said you could do it yourself but that it would be helpful to do it as a member of a small group or Job Cooperative. There is a great advantage to doing something with a group of peers, fellow-students, friends. Part of this value comes in knowing that others are doing the same kind of thing at the same time. Another is in knowing that others present are willing to help you if you have difficulty. Because there should be no criticism or judgment of what anyone says, but freedom to disagree, or even feel badly about the way it affects you, there will be affirmation of the best skills in each person. There will surely be some misunderstandings but you are all mature enough to survive those, especially when you accept the basic rule which is: *Each person has some kinds of excellence, and the purpose of the Co-op is to help each become aware of the skills and talents that combine to make that excellence a reality, with potential for improvement.*

Yet another value of working with a group is the fact that sharing your self-knowledge, especially your achievements, not only increases your own awareness of their hidden meanings but also their reality, and also earns you the respect of the others for what you've got. Other benefits include the opportunity to practice what to say at interviews, and the suggestions from others—who each make their own kinds of mistakes—on how to overcome and cope with the variety of problems that arise when life goes merrily on.

Motivated Skills Identification

In the first Co-op meeting share the earliest achievement you can remember. If there are ten of you, consider sitting in a circle and (going around the circle) talk one-by-one for a minute or less about the earliest achievement you can remember, preferably something you did before age ten. Then, in pairs with the partner next to you, share two achievements of the past five years, allowing a maximum of five minutes for each of you. Then working alone, you write out and organize your achievements. Even though you're working alone on this part, it is helpful to know that others are doing the same kind of task. In addition, if you get weary of writing and trying to remember, you'll find someone else in the group with whom to take a short break before getting back to the task.

These two sharings may seem unimportant, but you'll find they contribute substantially to a break with the traditions that hold back nearly everyone. They also help each person to bridge his way into the new process.

You will be moving along according to the instructions in Chapter One, identifying and numbering your seven greatest achievements. In that chapter it gives instructions both for taking the next step on your own and also for doing it with the help of a small group; but it is worthwhile to repeat the group, or Job Co-op, instructions here.

Get large sheets of paper, about double the size of pages in a large notebook, for each member of the Job

Co-op; butcher paper from your local meat market, cut in sheets about eighteen inches long, will do. You also need dark crayons or markers, for writing larger than usual—so others can look at it and read.

On that sheet, using your crayon or marker, list your five greatest achievements (five of the seven, so you can replace one if you feel you would rather not talk about that). No. 1 should be the achievement you feel is your greatest of all time—to date.

For this task work in groups of four or five. Each of you will take turns at reading his or her greatest achievements, then describing in detail what you did to make it happen. If there are five of you, number yourselves one to five and follow this process:

1. Hold up your list of five greatest achievements so the others can see it.
2. Read out your No. 1 Achievement, and describe what you did to make it happen. (You need to be detailed enough so that the others can identify most of the skills you used.)
3. Ask if the others have questions that will help them to be clear about the skills you must have used. (NOTE: Nobody is allowed to ask a "why" or a similar "curiosity" question that tries to "psych-out" the person upfront. If such a question is asked, the Upfronter can and should refuse to answer it.) The Upfronter should try to keep descriptions and answers short.
4. Repeat the process with Achievements Nos. 2, 3, 4 and 5.

After the Upfronter describes an Achievement, each of the others should write down on a clean page the skills each feels he or she must have used to make that experience happen. So each of the listeners develops a list of three or more skills under the numbers 1, 2, 3, 4 and 5 of the Achievements described by the Upfronter. It takes a lot of listening to hear what those skills are, but listening in this way gives you training in listening to what happens at job interviews.

When the Upfronter has finished the listeners read out—in turn—the skills they wrote down for all five, then pass their lists to the Upfronter.

Then each of the others, in turn, take the Upfronter position and the process is repeated. It usually takes about 15 minutes to complete an Upfronter experience.

WARNING! It is sure that *some* of the skills listed by the listeners are *not* accurate. The listeners could only guess at those skills, since they are not specially trained in identifying them. Also, the listeners will have overlooked some skills the Upfronter feels should have been obvious. They are also likely to have mentioned some the Upfronter did not think of as skills, a "normal" situation which shows we take some of our best skills for granted. The special helpfulness of the listeners is that their lists and comments stimulate the Upfronter to do a more thorough job of examining his Achievements and identifying the skills they show. Chapter Two gives the steps you should take to complete—on your own—that skills identification.

But members of the Job Co-op can help you to re-examine the skills you finally identify, and also practice talking about these motivated skills. They also help you to develop your Job Power Report—as described in detail in Chapter Three. Here is an outline of how the Co-op works first on your Job Power Report and then on interview practice.

The Job Power Report is your key tool for creating good interviews. It lists your motivated skills, and may offer some proof of their level of development. Because you were an Upfronter, three or four others deeply appreciate what you have to offer, and they can help you improve your report—if anyone can. So have a session with your team of four or five after each of you has written your Job Power Reports. Take turns in discussing your different Reports, and in giving proof of the skills you mention. Almost always someone will come up with suggestions, maybe criticism, that puts new light on what you have written; occasionally you'll say things differently, rewrite, or add or subtract items.

To take an extreme example, suppose your Report refers to outdoor skills and physical endurance. They could be stated these ways:

1. All the newspapers headlined and printed pictures of me as "Athlete Of The Year."
   OR the Report could say:
2. My outdoor skills and physical endurance are very good.

An interviewer reading the first one needs to ask no questions, perhaps would be impressed, but might think "This one sure likes the spotlight." The second example stimulates an interviewer to ask for evidence of your outdoor skills and physical endurance. If you then quietly said, "I was selected as Athlete Of The Year for my performances in track, football, javelin throw and tennis," there is no doubt about your impression on the interviewer. He then might think, "This guy is even better than it says here: I admire his modesty."

But whatever suggestions your Co-op team members give, you must take final responsibility yourself for what is in your Job Power Report. For instance, here's an example of how their advice could be harmful.

A woman artist broke her arm, her drawing arm. It

wasn't set right, so after two months it had to be set again, and it was slow in healing. She was out of practice for six months, and she knew she was slower than she should be. She protected herself in her Job Power Report by stating: "I sketch very well, and learn fast; but I'll be faster when I fully recover from a recent accident."

Her Co-op team told her she shouldn't be apologetic in her Report. But the way she thought about it was this: "If I get a job where they expect me to work very fast, which I ordinarily can do, I might not meet my employer's expectations. It would be better if I could be faster than they expect, and have a little extra time to do better quality work. Besides, if they ask me about the accident as well as for samples of my drawings, they'll be both sympathetic and understanding of my situation. They'll be more on my side when it comes to getting out a lot of work in a short amount of time." She checked her thoughts with a specially trained leader of Job Co-operatives, and made up her mind to keep the report the way she wrote it—and it worked.

In any case, all suggestions given during the Co-op meetings are intended to be helpful to each person, to recognize and affirm the best in each member, to help him overcome obstacles and reach his goal. So each meeting has as its central guide a spirit of helpfulness. That's a good, comforting and encouraging climate to be in. Once in a while we all need a supporting environment like that.

You'll find a list of frequently-asked interview questions at the end of Chapter Four, *Interviews, More Interviews.* You should use these and other questions you can think of in the practice sessions of your Co-op.

At your follow-through meetings, when you tell what happened at your interviews, be prepared to be told that you forgot some of what you learned at earlier practices. At that point, the thing to do is practice, or role play, some more. When you act-out what happened at an interview you usually can see more clearly the things you did right, some of the things you missed doing, and some things you might do to recover lost ground or to do better the next time.

Summary

The Job Cooperative is a means by which each member gets personal and group help in remembering, writing down and studying those experiences that reveal the pattern of skills and talents which combine to make up his unique excellence. It also helps each member to develop his Job Power Report, and practice what to say in order to create interviews and be effective at them. It is especially useful in researching the working world, helping all members to know how successful men and women got their starts, and in creating opportunities for Co-op members.

The next chapter, The Job Campaign, reveals another area where Co-op membership is worthwhile.

Win
Your Job
Campaign

6

*"Let your light so shine before men that
they may see your good works. . . . "*
from Sermon On The Mount

THERE ARE TWELVE STEPS in winning a job campaign. You have already completed the big ones, the first
six steps: 1) writing down, classifying and studying your
greatest achievements; 2) identifying your inner-motivated
skills or talents; 3) charting, rechecking and reality-testing
them; 4) using the facts you developed to write your Job
Power Report; 5) making a list of beginning contacts for
your campaign; 6) practicing what to say at your referral
and your job interviews.

Now come the tasks of the campaign strategy, which
put what you have learned into practice. These six steps
move much faster. They are:

1. making your contacts
2. having interviews and keeping records about them
3. writing thank you letters
4. letting your contacts know how you're doing
5. having job interviews, and
6. negotiating for your starting pay and for a pay
   increase

The key ways to make contacts and have successful
interviews without turndowns have been detailed in

Chapter Four. We'll summarize them again, and also point up the contact and interview system given in the Job Cooperative chapter.

You'll need a small notebook, one you can easily carry in your pocket. Rule off six spaces, one for each weekday and one for Saturday/Sunday, on each of the first ten pages; put day and dates at the top of each space. This is your Contacts Calendar, a way of keeping track of what you do and what you intend to do. The great majority of people who use this campaign strategy can expect to land jobs within six weeks, maybe even in the first week. This time is shortened when you work with a Job Cooperative. The other pages of your notebook are for making notes on the interviews you have and what you do about them.

The Contacts Calendar is the way you schedule what you want to do, what you have done, and the events and changes that take place. It's a kind of scoreboard. And as you know, when you start any game a scoreboard helps you to know how you're doing.

Not everyone uses a Contacts Calendar, and the process will work without it. It just works so much better with it that we especially recommend it. We believe you know that a car can run without oil, especially if you stop every few miles and let the engine and parts cool down. Your Contact Calendar, like oil, helps you to be sure that the job campaign is operating smoothly and on schedule, and that you have control of the changes you want to make.

You'll need your hundred Job Power Reports, the card on which you've written your Social Security number and other facts that go into job application forms (perhaps you should have two of these cards, and staple one inside the back of your notebook). And you should consider having a self-confidence and "staying cool" card. This is a 3x5 index card with a few words about your top three achievements on one side, and on the other side very short reminders of a couple of views which have given you feelings of happy peacefulness. This card is something you should look at, read and relax with for a few minutes before you have interviews. It has an important physiological effect—enabling you to take a deep breath, fill your body with a little extra oxygen, and become less tense. (If you don't want to carry that second card, you should take three or four deep breaths before you have an interview).

Another Hiring Viewpoint

Perhaps we should tell you about the employment game from the executive viewpoint, the viewpoint of the employer. It isn't really a game, but it often is spoken of as a gamble. When you know the rules, you can make the most of them; but if you don't know the rules, you can win only by accident. And the way employment is set up, the rules are kept very secret. First, an executive with a critical mass of money and equipment decides to make a profit by using them to provide a new product or service. To make it available he needs many different kinds of employees: executives, assistants, professional and technical men and women, record keepers of various kinds, typists, messengers, porters, etc.

Let's say that in his far-off headquarters he decides to build a new factory with a scientific testing laboratory and office in your small city. He arranges to get a low-interest loan and tax exemption for a number of years from your state and city in return for bringing his operation there. He first needs construction labor, a few construction clerks and timekeepers. The word about those jobs goes out usually through building trades unions, superintendents and foremen. Almost all the better jobs are filled that way. Then some more are filled by employees bringing along buddies and sons or daughters just in case there might be openings they could fill. A few are filled by persons who hear about the new construction job and drop by to see if there might be openings. And the remainder (about one in five) are recruited through newspaper ads, the Employment Security Office and employment agencies.

As the building nears completion machinery and equipment of all kinds, together with office supplies, arrive and are put into pre-planned places. Executive staff and some lower-level personnel arrive from headquarters, and hiring begins on a serious basis for daily operations. As higher-level persons get their jobs, they are asked to recommend others for lower-level jobs. The top boss knows that hiring mistakes will be made, and that some new employees will only last a week or two, others will stay for a few months, others will become regulars. And all the while the new people hired will be asked to recommend others who are needed.

Now here is how the hiring process begins. The top people are likely to be recommended through members of the local Chamber of Commerce, Rotary, political leaders, the Business and Professional Women's Club or other women's organizations, local professional, business and service clubs. These are the first groups that get news of a large hiring activity.

Every applicant is asked to complete a job application form, but for some of them it is after they have been hired. The person doing the hiring is almost never the employment or personnel manager, but a large number of applicants do get interviewed by someone in the personnel department; that's where you get screened out, or stopped from entering the employment process. The persons who come in through public and private agencies and newspaper ads generally get their first interviews in the personnel department.

Personnel people are usually aware of the decision as

to the kind of impression the new company wants to make. And it is customary for each interviewer to interpret differently what that impression means in regard to the kinds of persons who are employed. Some might like long hair, some have a bias against women in pantsuits, some want everyone to speak perfectly, some feel that high school and college dropouts are no good, some are partial to those with chemistry courses, some don't like blacks and other colored persons, some don't like persons over forty, some are partial to dark-haired persons and others to light-haired ones. There are any number of prejudices—we all have them in some degree—hidden in the personnel office and often without clear knowledge by the people who have these prejudices. They do exist even though they violate Equal Opportunity laws.

When you pass the first hurdle in the employment office you get referred to a supervisor or manager. He or she has responsibility for getting certain work done. If you can help him get that done, or if he believes you can, you will be hired. But he knows he must guess, on the basis of your past history, your studies, grades and perhaps recommendations from your teachers—and occasionally from psychological tests—whether you will be able to help him. He usually will hedge his guess by saying you'll be on probation for thirty days, ninety days, or 12 months. Then you get to talking about pay rates or salary, and it is customary for the starting rate to be a fixed one for beginners.

That's about the way it is from the employer's end

What you need to do in your job campaign is recogni how you can take advantage of what we've just told you. It is clear, to begin with, that you're more likely to get a job if you are recommended to an executive or supervisor. Nearly eight jobs out of ten are obtained that way, and only two out of ten are known right off to the personnel department and through ads and agencies.

You will notice that a business operation has a schedule for doing things. But the same principle applies with any organization. In fact, scheduling is mentioned in the Bible in relation to the construction of a house. Scheduling something means keeping track of what is going on, and knowing and deciding what things should be done first. It should even be clear that you cannot change your mind about what comes first until after you've made up your mind.

More on Contacts

You need ignorance in order to make good contacts. Most teenage men and women believe they have no contacts, and by that they mean they don't know where the job openings are. Knowing about job openings is one kind of ignorance. Knowing that you don't know if someone else knows about job openings, that's the kind of ignorance you need. If you think you know someone who wouldn't know of any job openings, then you're getting too smart. Everyone who buys or sells or gets anything repaired has contacts that can lead to job openings.

The way to reach those contacts, and get referred to other persons who might have contacts, is given in detail in Chapter 4, *Interviews, More Interviews.* We'll summarize those instructions here, and add an idea.

First, you can avoid being turned down by never asking for a job. Instead, tell your contact that you don't *expect* him to have a job or to know of one that would use your skills. What you want from him is some advice on your Job Power Report. Does he think it tells things about you that would interest an employer?

This process nearly always gets the person involved in knowing about you and advising you. It frequently influences him to ask you some questions about yourself—based on your Report. Then, to suggest one or two persons that he either would like to show your Report to or that you should see. If those suggestions are not made, you will need to ask if he knows someone who might be interested in having a copy of your Report, or a person who—although he is unlikely to have a job for you—occasionally hears of job openings. Either way, three out of four people you approach along these lines will give you at least one more referral. This means that if you make ten contacts on your own, you will gain between seven and twelve more from them; and those seven will lead to at least another five, and those five to at least another three—making a total of 25 from your original ten.

Now it takes time to have these R & R interviews, which is another reason why you need your Contacts Calendar. It helps you to keep track of who you see, when you saw them, and who you are to see in the future.

Each time you see someone and are questioned about your Job Power Report, you have influenced that person to remember you, and to keep you in mind if he or she hears of a possible job you could have. This makes them your allies in the job hunt because they are looking even though you are making the actual contacts. When someone is helping you in this way they deserve your gratitude; so you should send each of them a short note of thanks. It helps you in more than one way. First, it shows you appreciate their helpfulness and encourages them to remember you; second, it can keep them informed on how you are progressing; third, it can stimulate them to get in touch with you and give you some more contacts—even though you shouldn't ask for them.

This is the kind of "thank you" letter to write:

```
Dear Mr. (or Ms.) Blank:

I really do appreciate your help with my Report,
and especially your introduction to Mr. So-and-so.
I'll be seeing him next Tuesday.  And I'll write
you again in about two weeks and let you know
how I'm doing.
                              your name/address
```

A letter or postcard like that will take less than two minutes to write, so don't make excuses—as many people do—by telling yourself you've got too many other things to do so you don't have the time to write it.

Your job campaign, if you want to win it fast, is a full-time job that needs seven or eight hours a day of work five days a week and sometimes weekends. You'll need to make contacts, put appointments in your Calendar, make notes on what happened at your interview, keep more appointments and have more interviews, write letters, make telephone calls, sometimes feel very disappointed or even depressed when your efforts don't produce immediate results, get over your depression and go to work on your campaign again.

Nearly all people who are job hunting need company some of the time, someone to exchange ideas with, someone who will support and encourage you when things look dark. There are three kinds of "company" which are beneficial. The best is a Job Cooperative; next best is a group of three or more people like yourself who are also looking for jobs, especially if you all are using this system; third, and still very good, is family or an older friend with whom you feel comfortable.

Job Interviews

In the contact or R & R interview you were trying to get the person to hear your skills, remember you, and recommend you to another contact. The time comes, often after ten and usually by the time you've had thirty interviews, when you are interviewed for a job opening. Then you must change your approach. You are being interviewed for a job when an interviewer says something like this: "I have a job that could use your skills," or, "I'd like to get you into our beginners' training program." Your concern then is not how to be remembered and referred, but how to get a firm job offer with a starting date and rate of pay. Change tactics and start asking questions that get job facts. First of all say something like this: "I'd like to work in your organization. It seems like there will be opportunity to develop my skills and get ahead. Can you tell me just what this job requires?"

You need to listen carefully and answer your interviewer's questions constructively. Because you have thoroughly studied yourself, and have plenty of facts about what you can do in your Career Journal, you have the facts you need to know for a good interview virtually on the end of your tongue. So you can afford to listen carefully. Make some notes (in a notebook that should be with you at all kinds of interviews). Remember that you can't write and listen completely at the same time, so check the correctness of your notes with your interviewer.

Listening carefully, and asking questions about what you are not sure of, makes a very good impression at job interviews. It shows you might listen to instructions, and make fewer mistakes than others who might *not* listen so carefully. It shows you try to understand, and are willing to ask questions when you are not sure.

If the job is what you want, you should ask (and write down correctly) the name and title of the person who would be your supervisor. You should also ask when they would want you to start, and the starting rate of pay. Make a note of those items, too. And don't overlook asking when the working day begins and ends; you might otherwise be late or too early on the first day. Because an increasing number of organizations have what is called "flextime," you could ask if the organization permits earlier and later starts and stops for the day's work.

There are plenty of questions that employers often ask, and a list of these is given in the interviews chapter. You'll also find there a list of some questions you should consider asking.

When you are asked about your skills in a job interview, with a suggestion something like this: "Why don't you tell me something about your skills?"—be careful. Take a good breath (which relaxes your tension), and reply along these lines: "Would you like me to start with examples of my handskills, or my skill in persuading people, or my skill in organizing?" (You would use three important skills you mention in your Job Power Report.)

The employer would then either suggest one, or say "Start wherever you like."

And you either repeat the one he suggests, and speak clearly but briefly about the best experience you had which proves that skill; or you say, "All right, I'll start with my skill in organizing. It's a beginning skill, but this is what I've done which proves I have it." Then you go on with your experience, but be brief (not quick-speaking). After that, the employer will probably suggest you talk about some other skills, or else you name another skill and give another experience which proves it. It's true you have most of those things on your Job Power Report, but many supervisors like to hear the person speak about his own experiences.

Usually within twenty minutes the point will be reached where the employer either offers you the job, suggests that he'll let you know in a few days, or turns you down. If you're offered the job he'll talk about salary or pay rate, (see Chapter 4) and when you get started on the job. Let's deal with what to say if he's to let you know in a few days, and what to do if your interview is with a personnel or employment officer of an organization.

Your response to the "few days" comment should go like this: "I'd like to enter this in my calendar; if I don't hear from you by about Wednesday (make it three or four days away), would you mind if I called you about when you'd want me to start?" Nearly all the time you'll either get a "yes" to that or an explanation for a longer delay. Then you get the supervisor's telephone number and enter his name and number in your Calendar on the day when you should call him if you haven't heard. Another way you might respond is by asking if he would want you to be interviewed by someone else, now or at another time. If the reply is "yes" in this case, be sure to inquire and write down the name of the person who would be interviewing you on the next occasion. This could lead to his trying to arrange an immediate second appointment before you leave; and otherwise, it could lead to his suggesting that you call the other person to arrange the appointment.

If your interview is with "Personnel," the chances are that you are being screened for an interview with someone else. In this kind of situation the job of the interviewer is to make a judgment as to whether or not it is worthwhile for the supervisor to spend time with you. The interviewer does not have power to hire you, but does have power to reject you or to pass you through to the person with the positive power. So you want to make the earliest possible link with that positive power.

Your line with the personnel interviewer could be, after perhaps speaking about one or two skill-proving experiences, "Are you screening me for a job in another department?" And after you get your reply you might say, "Could you tell me who would be interviewing me in that department?" Try to be sure of the spelling of that person's name, and write it in your notebook. When you've done that, you'll have linked yourself with the final interviewer who has power to say "you're hired."

Now for the salary question. In the interviews chapter we said that employers almost always have basic starting rates of pay, and also that they are nearly always willing to hire good persons above that basic rate. Another thing to know is this: Most jobs have a pay rate with 30% difference between the highest and lowest rate of pay. This means that a job with a starting rate of $3.25 an hour is likely to have a top rate of about $4.15 an hour. On a weekly basis of 40 hours the figures are $130.00 and $166.00. If you are able to present your motivated skills while other applicants do not, the employer knows more surely how valuable you are to him and how valuable you are likely to be. So he can afford to pay you more than ordinary beginners—at least another ten percent, and perhaps even more than that.

If you don't ask for it, there's little reason for him to give it to you. As Chapter 4 suggests, you should feel comfortable about negotiating for it; or if you can't get it that way you should ask for an early review of your work, your worth, and what you are being paid. You really should be able to get a commitment of an early pay increase on the basis of good and dependable work.

If an employer turns you down, thank him. No good employer likes to turn down a good job applicant, so a turn down is painful to an employer and also shows he feels the job is wrong for you. This could mean that he knows of one that might be right for you. But you'll never get to know about it if you let yourself feel bad and slink away.

When you get turned down, try to tell the truth about your disappointment and then try to turn the situation around. If you can negotiate that turn-around you'll have a respecting friend in the employer and very likely a good lead to a better job. You could think along these lines, and say: "I guess you can see I'm disappointed that you don't want me, Mr. Jones. I suppose that's because you think the job isn't right for me or I'm not right for your organization. So I can't blame you for turning me down. But now that you've interviewed me, and gotten to know me, maybe you can think of some other place that could use my skills. I'd welcome any suggestion, and appreciate it."

We know that's tough to say when you've been hit by rejection. But if it makes sense to you, as we know it does, why not try practicing it? If you're in a Job Co-op, you'd be sure to get some help then. You could act out a scene with another Co-op member taking the part of an employer who's going to turn you down, and then see what he says after you try out what we suggested. You could do that just with a friend, too, but the Co-op is a continuing operation that will give you opportunity to test out things like this.

The employer who turns you down when you made so much effort feels he has hurt you. And that feeling makes him willing to do something to compensate for the hurt. If you give him the opportunity, by letting him off the hook and asking him for a referral, he's likely to come through to salve his own conscience.

The First Offer

You don't have to accept the first offer that's made to you. And you don't have to turn down a lousy job offer. If that first offer comes almost immediately after you start your campaign, try to put it on ice for three or four days—unless conditions are too rough for you. That amount of time will permit you to look into possibilities for other jobs, some of which may be better opportunities. The same timing problem can occur if you get a lousy job offer. Here's how to deal with it.

The employer who makes a lousy job offer is either trying to do you a favor (which he may not be able to afford) or he knows he's offering you a lousy job. Either way, he'll be willing for you to take a little time to decide about getting started. So you could consider saying something like this: "I know this is a starting job and that maybe it could lead to something better. I would like to think about what it could lead to and would like you to keep that job for me for just a few days. Is that okay?" Then ask for four or five working days to think about it and talk it over with some friends.

In the meantime, contact as many people as you can (including those you've seen before) using the R & R Interview system. Tell them you have been offered a job but you would prefer something that comes closer to one that would use your skills. And could they refer you to someone during the next couple of days who might hear of or know of a job that you might like.

Believe us, there's nothing so electrifying to a person as the idea of helping someone who already is a success— has already been offered a job. Your contacts will, most of them, call their friends and write to them about you. They'll give you introductions. They'll do everything possible to help make bigger your success in finding a job. And there's a good possibility that they'll be successful within the four or five days—so you'll be able to accept another new offer and tell the old one two things: first, you accepted a better job offer and second, that if he doesn't mind you'd like to see if you could recommend someone else for his job. What seems to be a lousy job to you might appear to be a good one to someone else. Then you could turn that first offer over to a friend, or to the Job Cooperative if you are a member of one.

There is another alternative on that "lousy" job offer. You could send your Job Power Report to about thirty organizations and ask if they have an opening for your skills. A cover letter to go with your Report would read something like this:

```
Dear Sir:

I have carefully studied my experience and identi-
fied which skills are most likely to be successful
and satisfying for me and my employer.  The job
which I've been offered fails to make use of them.

You will find them on the attached Job Power Report.
Will you please read it and let me know who might
want to use them.

I'll be waiting for your call.  And thank you for
considering me.

Yours truly,

John Jones
Tel. 123-4566
99 West First St.
Jackson, Colo.  61434
```

A letter like this can be printed in the same way that you did your Job Power Report, so all you'd have to do is sign it and put it into an envelope addressed to the heads of organizations in your city or community. You can get the names of these executives through your local Chamber of Commerce, the nearest Business and Professional Women's Association, with the aid of someone in Service Clubs like Rotary, or, particularly, with the help of your local librarian who probably has a listing of these executives. Pick out about thirty, hand address the envelopes and be sure to put the right amount of postage on them. Because this will enable you to be thirty places at once, in the next day or two, no later than the third day, you should be getting telephone calls. Jobs won't be offered over the telephone, but you're likely to get some job interviews which could lead to offers.

You can follow a very similar procedure to deal with a job offer that comes right at the start of your campaign. If you can get the employer to hold that job for you while you talk about it with some friends and advisors, perhaps you'll have time enough to test out the possibility of getting additional offers with some of your other contacts—just as was suggested in regard to the lousy job offer.

Either way, one thing is certain—you don't have to stay in a job if it is a dead end. The strategies given in this book enable you to make contacts, create contacts, even get potential employers to telephone you. Because good employees are not easy to find, employers usually are willing to window-shop your skills after work and during weekends and lunch periods. In addition, it is possible that a job you feel is a dead-end could turn out to have good possibilities. For instance, one young man of 17, who was unemployed and sick of dead-end cafeteria porter and dishwashing jobs, studied his achievements and found out that his skills belonged in the restaurant field—but he had potential for being a manager. Here's the first paragraph of the Job Power Report he wrote:

```
Potential Restaurant or Cafeteria Manager, willing
to start at the bottom as dishwasher or porter and
learn every operation.  I can prove I am very ob-
servant, have some experience working with foods,
service and cafeteria cleanliness, have lots of
physical endurance, get along well with all kinds
of people, have a good memory and work O.K. with
figures and records.
```

The first afternoon he got his Report copies he tested it out with four restaurants in areas where he didn't want to work; he got four job offers. That happened after he had been unemployed for two months. Then he went to his own area and four days later accepted employment with a cafeteria chain.

Every beginner in a job should have assurance of a first pay increase. But it should be dependent on doing a good job, not just sticking around without being a nuisance. You can get that assurance during your first few days on the job.

Here's what do do, and why it is reasonable.

As soon as you find out who your real boss is, the person who can recommend you for a pay raise that you'll get, find an opportunity to speak to him alone for a couple of minutes. Say something like this to him: "I want to do a good job here, Mr. Smith, and I'd like a little help from you. Will you keep an eye on me to make sure I'm learning, and when I make mistakes tell me about them in time to correct them before it's too late? I'd really appreciate that, Mr. Smith." He's sure to agree if he has any time at all for you, and he should have. Then you say, "After a month or two, when you see I'm doing o.k., will you give me a raise?" While Mr. Smith may balk a little about the time factor, he's almost sure to agree with the general idea that when you have proved you're doing good work you should get a raise.

After you get started you should thank your new employer, in writing, for the job. You could write something like this:

Dear Mr. Brown:

Thank you for the job I started three days ago. I have a lot to learn, and I shall be following instructions and doing the best I can. I appreciate the pay of $130.00 weekly, and especially the idea that when I prove I am capable for a month or two I'll be considered for a raise. I want to get ahead and show you can depend on me.

Yours truly,

You should also thank all the contacts you made, because that will get them in a mood to help you in the future if you need their help. So write them a letter along these lines: "Your helpfulness has now resulted in my getting a job with the (name and organization), where I started (give date). I do want you to know that I appreciate your advice and the contacts you gave me. Yours truly . . . . ." And that's the end of a good job finding campaign.

Summary

The way to win your job campaign is to get interviews without turndowns, keep records and a schedule of what you are doing and what you have agreed to do, survive the blues when you feel that progress isn't fast enough. When you get interviewed for a job listen carefully, negotiate on salary and when you are to start working, decide whether or not to accept a job offer, and set a date for your first pay increase.

Maintain
Your Progress

7

---

*"Greatness knocks at every door, but it is usually
double-barred by old beliefs, pride of opinion."*
Noral Holm

JUST AS YOU GET HUNGRY AGAIN several hours after
a good meal, once you've digested your job you'll want something more interesting and challenging. Growth and progress require change for the better. In the working world these
have traditionally been visible as pay increases and promotions. But the modern world we live in, and the one we are
moving toward, are giving new meanings to "change." Just
the increased pace of change has altered its impact. Jobs
are becoming obsolete, and new jobs are being invented, at
an ever faster rate. Some organizations require employees
to handle a variety of jobs, and to change duties and responsibilities from time to time. In some organizations, special task forces are set up to get certain things done from
time to time, and the leader of a task force one day may become just another member of a different task force another
day. In different organizations there are five-day workweeks, four-day workweeks and three-day workweeks. And
"flextime" permits employees in some organizations to
start and end their workdays earlier or later than the usual
8 or 9 a.m. to 4 or 5 p.m.

Because of what you know about yourself as a result of
working through this book, you can choose to manage these

changing circumstances rather than letting them manage you. A high proportion of men and women drift along as changes occur, and pay the price of drifting—with frustration and more serious problems, including occasional unemployment. In 1979 more than 23 million men and women were unemployed at some time or other, not counting about two million more who had given up looking for jobs. The problems that arise are not only those of meeting expenses, but can be psychological too. Thoughts occur such as, "My life has lost its meaning," and "Nobody wants me," and, "I've become a nobody," and "There's nothing to my life any more," and "The system has put me on the outside; I don't belong."

Those feelings are real enough, but you don't have to have them if you choose to manage your circumstances. This requires that you keep track of how your potential is growing, set goals, plan for what you want and be prepared to increase or reduce your objectives. Also, you will need to develop a support system of other people and establish and maintain personal relationships. In addition, you will need to be aware of circumstances that are changing and the signs of new changes. The rest of this chapter is about how to do all these things, and how you can prepare to benefit from the flow of progress that might otherwise pass you by.

The basic work of this has already been completed in your Career Journal. A little effort is required to maintain it, but before going into that let's look at some of the realities of the 1970's. About ten years ago there was a military contract cutback and tens of thousands of space scientists and engineers suddenly found their jobs were obsolete. The most successful government-sponsored program to help them change jobs and careers was an experimental one directed by Bernard Haldane in the U.S. Department of Labor headquarters. A majority of the 22 people in this project got jobs with equivalent pay within two months, and more than 80 percent had jobs a few months later. Nearly all said that by using the systems described in this book they regained their self-confidence and many changed their careers successfully.

Bridging

It is extremely important to have a handle on your best skills, so you can change the way they are combined and bridge your way to fit new and different requirements in the job market. One young person who learned to do this was Alex Jones, a twenty-year-old Vietnam veteran, home after two years of service. He'd been promoted in the field three times and then had led his squadron; he'd been busted three times when he returned behind the lines, and had seen the inside of jail twice. He received honorable discharge as a private. He was a high school dropout who completed his equivalency tests while in the Army, and was awarded two medals.

When Alex came to a Bernard Haldane project the Army was sponsoring, he resisted participation at first. As a black man, he'd had his share of being pushed around. After persistent counselor encouragement he told how he had, at the age of nine, organized kids to keep paths and sidewalks clear of snow, on a contract basis. He kept this business going for two years and made a lot of money. Before getting started he had studied five years of weather information for his area to find out how much snowfall he could expect. He had also checked what people paid other kids for clearing away snow. Then he worked out a snow season contract, lined up twenty kids to work on an hourly basis as needed, and solicited neighborhood residents for the business on a guaranteed basis. Later, in high school, he had organized another small business, and again in the Army. Each time the task required sensing a need or getting the idea, studying possibilities and prices, recruiting and organizing his "employees," and selling the service.

As he remembered these experiences, he quickly perceived that his best skills—going back to childhood—included management, organizing and marketing. He then found himself with the choice of becoming a guerilla-type leader (on the streets), with all the uncertainties and possibilities involved, or trying for management in a good private company where his skills were also needed—but where good pay and increasing opportunities could be developed with reasonable certainty. He never before had seen that second option. He said that was because while he knew he was a leader he had not been aware of his management and marketing skills. Our project had helped him to get a handle on his best skills and change his attitude from frustration about lack of dependable opportunity into perception of it.

This is an example of what is sometimes called "bridging." When you know what your best skills and talents are, you are better able to bridge your way—through changing how your skills are combined—to a different or improved career that continues to give you growth opportunity and fulfillment. Knowledge of how to "bridge," and what you have to bridge with, takes much of the fear out of progress and change. But the facts of your job and talents change from week to week and month to month—you get better at some things; you read a book that gives new insights; you meet someone whose challenge causes you to gain a new viewpoint; you complete a course, seminar or training program; you get to know better some person who can influence your career development.

You need to be aware of how your job is changing and your talents are growing. The way to do that is to keep track of important events related to your career. A loose leaf Career Progress Book (about 5.5 x 8.5"), and three sheets from it in your pocket, make a tool for progress available to you at all times. This Progress Book augments your Career Journal. Develop the habit of using it each week. Sometimes you can write as little as one line a week, perhaps "Nothing much happened last week." At other times you will be able to report to yourself that you were assigned a new responsibility or task, or that you met a major department head for the first time—and that you seemed to hit it off. Sometimes you might write in your Progress Book that a movie you saw, a book you read, or a conversation you had gave you the key to solving a problem; an additional task could open the door to perceiving a whole new world; you might recognize the wisdom of learning to use the typewriter, or avoid using it; you might complete a task, save a particular sum of money, buy something you long wanted; you could get your own apartment or decide to share one; you might start or finish a training program or decide you need to get to know someone better.

Because your job or career is the largest single segment of your life, it affects all the rest of it. And the reverse also is true. So your Career Progress Book has entries that are both personal and job-related. When you make entries every week (some find that too hard, and do it once a month, but more often is better) you will soon be able to observe your up and down cycles which we all have. You could choose to ignore them, but ignoring them cuts off your ability to use them. When you get to know your cycle times of high creativity and productivity, for instance, you can often shift routine and riskless activities to low cycle times and use high cycle times for activities requiring more creativity and energy. But that's only one benefit which can come from keeping track of your progress. We have daily and monthly cycles of energy and effectiveness, and your Progress Book can help you to identify them.

Now that you know your best skills, talents and strengths, it is easier for you to set short-term and longer-term goals—and also to change them as you see fit. You cannot change your mind until after you've made it up; you cannot modify a goal or objective until after it is chosen. It is customary for people to set self-defeating goals; this gives evidence of their "humanity," fallibility enables them to feel sorry for themselves, and provides opportunity to indulge in the time-consuming effort of trying to learn from their mistakes.

That's the traditional approach that seemed to work well enough for centuries. But it's not the kind of goal setting we're talking about. We're suggesting that you set your goals and objectives for the short term, so you can quickly see results, how your strengths and your achievements relate to the way you want to grow. You can use a four-step formula to plan your progress over the next six months.

For the first step, use your imagination to take yourself six months into the future, and look back. Write down on a Career Progress page what you would like to look back on as having accomplished. Go into a fair amount of detail— savings, weekends away or vacation, relationships, leisure time activities, things to buy, job duties and responsibilities, etc. Dream it; see it as happening in your fulfilling life. At the start, dream as wild as you like.

The next steps bring this "dream" closer to reality. The second step is to flip your imagination to three months from now. What must you have done by then to be halfway toward your six-month goals? Write those activities down. Then re-examine your six-month goals and try to decide if they appear attainable. Where it seems they are not, because of circumstances only you can know about, modify them. This brings you closer to reality.

Third, come closer in your imagination to a time one month from now. What must you have done during that month to be a third of the way to your three-month goals? The detail here is likely to make you reconsider the feasibility of some of your three and six-month goals; where that happens, modify your goals again.

The fourth step is now. What must you do *now* to get started towards your goals? List those things as best you can, modify your one, three and six-month goals as you think best, and get going on what you must do in the next few days. But be sure, in addition, to keep a record of what you have done, what you have started.

When you develop these lists you possess a kind of barometer which you should check from time to time to find out how you are progressing toward your goals. At the end of the first month, you'll find you're progressing faster in some activities, and slower in others, than your original plan indicated. Then you should do a little more imaginative dreaming. Leap one month ahead and imagine what you would need to have done by that time to achieve your three-month objectives. The experience of your first month will influence you to make some changes, perhaps shortening the time for some goals, lengthening the time for others, maybe dropping some of the three- and six-month goals, maybe adding one or two based on your new circumstances.

When you deal with your realities and dreams in this way you can influence many circumstances, and take advantage of many situations that might otherwise bring you great frustrations and disappointments. Your "Six-month Goals" pages should be inserted at the back of your Career Progress Book. Each month you should look at your progress facts, "leap" forward a month and look back with your imagination, then modify or otherwise correct your goals again. At the end of six months you will find that doing this enables you to gain more fulfillment and progress than you previously thought was possible (Keep it up, and by the time you are in your mid-twenties or even sooner you may want to make 12-month and five or ten-year goal plans.)

Support System

You will find it easier to reach your goals if you work with a small group that meets regularly. A member of one group that has met regularly for three years, at first weekly for lunch and now once a month (sometimes by telephone conference), reports that all seven members have far exceeded their growth expectations. And they claim that a major cause for this kind of personal and career growth has been the climate of mutual support these meetings established. Each member is constantly concerned with the best for each of the others, each is alert to events, news and relationships that could help one or more of the others, and all the members know that each is unique and has a special kind of excellence.

We call this kind of recognition and mutual helpfulness a "Partnership of Excellence." And we suggest that you consider initiating your own group that can develop into a Partnership of Excellence. This is a working life (or college life) extension of the Job Co-op idea. You could start with seven to ten men and women about your own age, perhaps at your place of work, perhaps some members of your high school or college Job Co-op, perhaps including some from your neighborhood. At the beginning try to meet once each week at the same time, and do this for a least four weeks as a starting experiment. An hour should be long enough for the "business" part of this meeting, so it could be during lunch or at someone's house in the evening.

What you do at these meetings may seem too simple to many people, but it works: each of you takes a turn at relating your greatest achievement of the past week. As each person speaks, the others listen and may ask for further details on the activity (but no "why" questions) to gain clarity on what happened. For some, the activities presented will remind them of ways to help the person to have more fulfillment. Write those thoughts down. When all have had their say, go round your circle of partners and present your thoughts or helpful suggestions. Not everyone will have a helpful idea every time, but over several meetings it is likely that each one will be given some helpful ideas or introductions. Another thing to remember is this: when you meet on a weekly basis most achievements of the past week will be not very important, but occasionally one will be. And if you have written down your goals and objectives, you'll sometimes be able to speak of achieving one or more of those objectives.

What you will have in this "Partnership of Excellence" is a support group to help you cope with changes and difficulties, and also help you to achieve your objectives.

Work Relationships That Help You

Relationships in the work arena are important to your growth and progress. Doing a good job, and just keeping your nose to the grindstone, is usually the most dependable way to be ignored and overlooked. Supervisors are busy, and they are generally pleased to let well enough alone when effective work causes them no problems. They must give so much time to mistake-makers that they often don't have time to notice how good and unusual a job their best employees are doing. We've designed a simple system you can use to get around this very human condition of oversight.

As you know, you cannot get power until after you plug in to power lines. The power lines in the organization where you now work are relationships with people. You may not identify who they are immediately—it usually takes two months or more. When you get the power-line people to know you, learning and growth opportunities come more easily and you can avoid being overlooked. So one of your tasks is to identify the power-line people and their relationships to your advancement. You'll need one page for that, and about ten names, in your Career Progress book.

You sometimes have to look hard to find out how and where you can "plug in" to a power-lines person. One man who found the Assistant to the President unreachable, was able to make contact with him through the company library--since the Assistant was in charge of the library. For a young woman, access to a power-line person became possible because both of them were collectors of old shaving mugs. Usually the organization's chart of management responsibilities will give clues to where power-line people are likely to be, although a title and position on the organization chart often don't show how much power a person has. For new employees access to power-line people usually is through their assistants, secretaries, associates or relatives. Hobbies, athletic, church and community activities frequently provide access to power-line people.

You don't just go up to a power-line person and say "Hi, I'm Mary Brown in your production department." You first seek out ways to identify some of the person's background, interests and activities. Then one of the ways you might reach him is to get your own supervisor to let you deliver something to him. Or you might consider sending a carefully-worded note with an item of interest to him. For instance, suppose you find out that power-line person is really interested in trout fishing. Just once, when you spot something about trout in a newspaper or magazine, you could clip it and send it to him with a very short note along these lines: "I heard you might be interested in seeing this clipping. If I spot any more I'll send them along if you like." Then sign your name and give your section or department and phone number.

You must know about the person with power to block your advancement. Another one to know about is the person who can be most influential in getting you a promotion or a transfer from one department to another. A different power-line person may be the one who can help you get a pay increase.

You don't have to "brown-nose" or "polish the apple" of a power-line person in order to get ahead. You do have to play the "politics of productivity," or do the kind of job that brings you the reputation of being dependable. This means doing a good job where you are—being especially good when you are applying your motivated skills, and both putting up with and doing a reasonable job at other activities that are parts of your job. It also means keeping records of what you are doing, as we've said before, and occasionally bringing them tactfully to the attention of your immediate supervisor. This last task must also be done carefully. But you can be overlooked if you are reliably helpful rather than being difficult and requiring frequent supervision. So, as a dependable employee, you need to take some action that gets your reliability noticed.

Communicate

One easy way to communicate your reliability and progess is with the aid of your Career Progress Book. Toward the end of your first month in the working world, begin to summarize the most significant of your work-related achievements, especially as they have enabled your supervisor to be worry-free. You should try to get at least four, and up to ten items. Complete your list at the end of the month—either in clear handwriting or on a clean typed page (be sure to have a copy of it for yourself), then ask for a ten-minute appointment with your supervisor to discuss how you're doing. At that meeting tell her you're trying to keep a list of the best things you feel you've done. Say you'd like her to check it out with you and correct you where necessary so you can learn to do better. Then give her your list. If she fully agrees with you and says only, "you're doing fine; keep it up," you will at least have helped her to be aware of the activities in which you are doing best. Whatever more she says can only be helpful.

After doing this for a couple of months—during which time you'll also have an opportunity to get acquainted with several other people in the organization, including some power-line people—you will be ready to ask about the possibility of assignments or tasks that will get you a promotion. You can be sure that discussing these "reports on your effectiveness" with your supervisor will result in his thinking of you as an out-of-the-ordinary employee. A desired side-effect will be that your supervisor starts to speak about you with other supervisors and says, "he (or she) is a comer."

If you request advice from a power-line person about what you have to do to get a promotion, and tell him you have written these monthly reports, the power-line person is likely to ask for a copy. Give him a copy and keep one yourself, or else be sure to ask that it be returned. The power-line person may suggest another appointment in a week or so, and in the meantime check your reporting accuracy and look around for possible openings that could mean your promotion.

All that doesn't sound like very much to do, and it isn't. It doesn't take a lot of extra time. But it does require you to be alert to the sensitivities of the people around you, to get along with them, to keep records of your own actions, and to communicate clearly with superiors in your organization. Not everyone can or is willing to do all these things. But if you want to grow in your own way, and have greater fulfillment in what you do, these steps are much more dependable than the usual approach of "hoping for the best," or "letting nature take its course."

Your Skills Identity

When you are aware of the motivated skills that combine to make your skills identity and clarify your growth directions, you can strongly influence your own development. But not all the time. There will be changes in the structure of your organization: perhaps your supervisor will be promoted before he's had a chance to recommend you for promotion; or your entire department could be wiped out by a reorganization or a shift in location. You need to be ready for these changes, and prepared to take advantage of them. This means keeping your Job Power Report up to date, revising it about each six months until you've had some four years of experience. And it means letting your former contacts know about your progress every six months or so. This doesn't mean you're hunting another job, but it does imply that you are open to suggestions when the right opportunities come along. It also means that if you should lose your job for any reason you'll have a list of people to contact for future help.

It is very important to keep in touch with your skills identity. Another way to keep it very much alive is through a new computer matching system that can instantly relate what U.S. Labor Department officials call your job characteristics with those of specially analyzed job openings. The Department of Labor has been testing this system for several years, and expects to have it in every State Employment Security Office by 1985. While it has some limitations, it is over fifty percent more effective than present government placement techniques.

This computer system, called Manpower Matching Systems has a Job Analysis Vocabulary (JAV) and a Detailed Experimental Computer-Assisted Language (DECAL). These enable jobs to be categorized into 39 broad fields of work, and both applicants and jobs to be matched in greater detail than ever before. Key words are used to analyze jobs submitted by employers and to develop descriptions of individuals. The description includes a person's interests, aptitudes, temperaments, physical demands (e.g. can you work only in a damp climate), work conditions, education, trainings. These words are listed in a "thesaurus of occupational and educational descriptors." As job orders come in from employers, they are coded and put into a computer. The person registering with an Employment Security office is referred to a specially-trained interviewer, who describes his or her skills and traits and encodes them for the computer matching. When fully operating, Manpower Matching Systems will make it possible for you to wait while the computer tries to match your coded information in several different combinations against all jobs in its memory bank until a match is found. And it can keep working on this kind of matching as long as necessary, or just once for an "instant" job opening possibility.

Manpower Matching Systems is a new and most valuable development. At the present time it is necessarily centered on employer needs, and applicants who fit those needs. That's the way our economic system works, now. But an increasing number of men and women are becoming aware of the fact that this traditional view does not give sufficient consideration to the person, and that personal fulfillment in the world of work is possible. Manpower Matching Systems is an important movement in that direction, but it doesn't start with the person.

It is possible now, in the 1980's for individuals to present their job requirements based on motivated skills and obtain jobs that reasonably fit those skills. There's not much chance of a *perfect* match, but the less pleasing parts of a job can be reduced when the employer knows he will have a more effective and satisfied worker as a result of respecting the skills identity—the motivated skills pattern —of the person.

When you keep watch on yourself, your growth, and how your job changes or can change, you have a better chance to maintain the benefits derived from working through this book.

The United States has inherited traditional hiring practices from feudal and plantation times. Then, hiring and promotion for special tasks was by recommendation to the landowner. He made all the judgments about how well a person would do a job, and the person was rarely, if ever, consulted. Nobody thought the employee had any way of judging what he could do well. Employers today continue to take on themselves—as the old landowners—the task of judging who can do what and how well. Recommendations still account for 80 percent of the jobs filled. But the difference now is that the employee is not only better educated and able to talk and write about his experience, but he can also give the information that was missing: what he can do well and enjoyably, his motivated skills.

As our System to Identify Motivated Skills (SIMS) has gained increasing acceptance over the last fifteen years, doubts have disappeared about whether or not the person knows more about himself than the supervisor or employer. Regardless of what an employer says a person can do well, only the person knows which tasks or activities give him satisfaction and which don't.

Because you know your motivated skills, you can identify which tasks you are most likely to do well and enjoyably. You cannot make sure you have more of those activities in your work unless you discuss them with your employer from time to time. Both you and your employer will gain from that communication, because you will have more opportunity for growth and your employer will have opportunity to gain through better use of your skills. Already some employers are seeing these values, and encouraging their employees to identify their motivated skills. Smith Kline Corporation, the Atomic Energy Commission and Exxon are among the pioneers of this very new approach that can help all employees come closer to finding fulfillment through their work.

Manpower Matching Systems can increase its effectiveness by relying on applicants (not interviewers) to provide motivated skills information for translation into job-matching characteristics. But such radical modernization—with prime consideration for the personhood of applicants' needs rather than for the employers' needs—would require a serious policy change at the U.S. Department of Labor; after all, its budget is based on how many jobs it fills, rather than how many persons it gets into fulfilling jobs.

You will recall that we began this book by saying there is excellence in each person, and the skills-structure of that excellence starts to reveal itself early in life. You do expect some kinds of skills and talent to show early in music (Isaac Stern, Liza Minelli, Mozart) and athletics (Hank Aaron, Mark Spitz, Chris Evert). In mechanics, invention and aviation there are early achievers also: Henry Ford (he fixed clocks when he was 6), Igor Sikorsky, Thomas Edison. The early signs of later achievements are not only in these visible occupation people but also in everyone. Here are some more people whose lives prove it: Werner von Braun first built a working rocket when he was age 13. Euell Gibbons,

146

author of Stalking Healthful Herbs and other foraging books, created a candy bar of foraged hickory nuts and hackberries—when he was 5. You might already know about India's Prime Minister, Indira Ghandi's childhood. When she was about seven her favorite game with her family servants was to sit them in rows in the kitchen, stand on a table in front of them, and talk at them until she was too tired to speak. How's that as a start for a powerful politician! Then there's Houdini, the great magician. It's a fact that he played with locks and padlocks on chests, trunks, doors and boxes when he was a child of seven.

In the field of poetry, Robert Frost's first published poem appeared when he was twelve. In education, the son of an illiterate Argentine packtrain driver fell in love with learning and managed to read when he was four. Domingo Sarmiento opened more than 1,000 schools in his lifetime. In mathematics, a Swiss journal studied 93 leading mathematicians. It reported that 35 favored a math career before age 10, 43 before age 15, 11 more before age 18. Paul de Kruif studied 24 distinguished medical doctors. At an average age of 14 1/2, he says, medicine became a clear vocation for them. As final examples, take Grandma Moses, the artist whose works became famous after she reached 80. The first of her painting efforts started when she was 7, with sheep dip for paint. And take Malcolm X, who demonstrated his ability to talk and persuade others when he was 11.

Now that you've worked your way through this book you are not surprised by the stories about these famous people and their early starts. You know that you also have excellence in you, and that you can patiently pursue your own right to happiness by applying your motivated skills in your work and in other activities of your life. You also know that when you have problems and frustrations—they are a part of living and growing—you can immerse yourself in motivated skills activities. The strengths you express then will help you to cope with difficulties, surmount them or otherwise benefit from them. You can say to other jobless and troubled young men and women, as St. Paul did, "Stir up the gifts of God that are within you." Because you have done it, you know they can do it too, and you know the benefits that result from doing it."

Now that you know your lights, let them shine ever more brightly and be thankful.

Maybe that's too sermon-like an ending for this book, so here's another one. Very few people find their vocations in childhood. But virtually all children demonstrate skills that turn out to be career strengths later in life. Each person has some kind of excellence in him or her. Nobody is a "nobody." Each person is important in this world, and we all have the power to make an impression if we know the best that's in us and how to use it.

The path is not easy, but it is no more difficult than taking the traditional hit or miss approach to living. It takes less time, too, when you know what you've got, how you can change it, and where you're going. And the rewards are greater—more job satisfaction, more opportunity for growth, and usually more of the financial rewards if you should want them.

When you take the plunge into this new kind of self-understanding your new knowledge prevents you from kidding *yourself* any more. But perhaps the increased fullness of living that this knowledge lets you earn is worth that loss.

Appendix

A. Brief history of SIMS

B. Related Life Planning Theories

C. Book and Information Sources

D. Biographies of Authors

A Brief History of SIMS   A

BERNARD HALDANE developed SIMS (System to Identify Motivated Skills), starting in the 1940's when a wide variety of humanistic and behavioral sciences systems began. After studying psychological testing and labor relations at Columbia and New York Universities, and work as Labor Relations Consultant and Labor Editor of the New York Journal of Commerce, he was asked as a volunteer to develop a system to help World War II military officers capitalize on their military experience and find good jobs. Mayor Fiorello LaGuardia gave him space at 500 Fifth Avenue in New York City (now the home of Pepsi Cola), secretarial help, and space for all the management volunteers he could train. Nineteen such men and women he recruited and trained then helped over 2,500 officers in two years, ending in 1947. That's when he started Bernard Haldane Associates, Inc., now an international organization with professional counselors in forty major-city offices. A Harvard Business Review article in 1947 showed that Haldane's volunteer activities were considered valuable by 96 percent of the officers going through it and that nearly 80 percent were helped to bridge their way to better jobs and careers than the ones they held prewar.

For that work a commendation from The White House, the first of three, was delivered to Bernard Haldane in December, 1946. A different kind of commendation came in 1948 when, after leading a seven-week seminar at the Harvard Business School, Mr. Haldane's early systems became the backbone of that institution's first placement manual for alumni. Later that year, for the Society of Advancement of Management, he developed and led a placement program for its eleven student chapters in New York metropolitan area colleges and universities. A few years later, at the Bronx High School of Science, his research efforts were focused on developing procedures to help high school students identify their best talents and career goals. More experimentation at Rutherford (N.J.) and Haddonfield high schools sharpened his procedures, which proved highly effective with students at Madison Township high school and also in the women's Job Corps Center in Clinton, Iowa.

A third pioneering effort, re-employment programs for men and women due to lose their jobs because of employer shutdowns, technological changes and facility relocations, began in 1960 at the CBS Electronics plants in Danvers and Lowell, Mass. In a public statement, CBS said his work "headed off an unemployment crisis." Two years later, with the EXXON Corporation (then Standard Oil — N.J.), Bernard Haldane Associates contracted to assure reemployment within three months for at least 70 percent of those using his systems. Of 44 men and women in the initial EXXON program, in an area with over 9 percent unemployment, within a ninety day period 41 had new jobs paying within 10 percent of their previous salaries. This led to similar programs for many other companies and also to a fourth pioneering work—the renewal of self confidence and employability of persons long unemployed, dependent on public welfare, and over age 45. Nearly two-thirds of these "unemployables," taken out of the "dead files" of the State Employment Service, found jobs for themselves during the specially-designed two-month project. "It's a psychological miracle," said New Jersey Commissioner Raymond J. Male, in publicly announcing use of Haldane's system throughout the State.

Among the many leading organizations currently using the System to Identify Motivated Skills and methods based on it are Exxon, Union Carbide Corporation, The Peace Corps, the Atomic Energy Commission, Harvard Graduate School of Business Administration, Columbia University, SmithKline Corporation, the State of New Jersey, Xerox Corporation, all Church-related clergy counseling services, Universities of Hartford, Maryland, and many more.

During the last fifteen years Haldane projects have been designed and implemented to help beginning college students select courses that will develop their motivated skills, to train Defense Department Transition Project Counselors, to help S.E. Asian refugees become self-dependent, to help supervisors and employees jointly concerned with career planning and manpower utilization, to help teenage women locate jobs through YWCA programs, to enable clergy and religious workers adapt to the secular world of work, to help returning Peace Corps Volunteers integrate their service experiences with requirements of U.S. employment, to help women be career-assertive and self-confident, to help men and women in mid-career clarify their goals and be renewed in their work, through the Federal Women's Program—to help women get deserved career recognition, to change the self-image and employability of young ex-convicts, to help military persons, scientists, teachers and others change careers without loss of income, and to re-orient and modify the attitudes of potential high school dropouts. Seven years ago the District of Columbia Board of Education examined and accredited the Haldane systems for career and placement counseling of military personnel.

Many former employees and associates of Bernard Haldane have—in their own organizations—spread adaptations of SIMS. One who has obtained much publicity is

John Crystal who, in association with Richard N. Bolles, obtained grants from the Eli Lilly Foundation to take them into colleges across the country. Dick Irish and Eli Djeddah are some others, all four of whom have written books based on the Haldane systems. Tom Hubbard and Saul Gruner have spread the system into numerous corporations, national and international. Some better-known authors who have commented favorably on Haldane's work are Vance Packard, Dr. Norman Vincent Peale, Auren Uris, Martin L. Gross, Malcolm Kent, and Columbia University's director of placement counseling—Richard Gummere. Haldane's basic techniques, especially adapted for clergy with mid-career problems, were given to the Northeast Career Center of the United Presbyterian Church, then headed by Rev. Thomas Brown; this career center has since birthed a dozen similar ecumenical centers across the country. Bernard Haldane has also helped to modernize the procedures offered through the 40-plus clubs, Man-marketing clinics, and the Job Finding Forum in New York City.

During the last eight years Jean Haldane has made numerous contributions to development of the Haldane systems, particularly in the areas of group dynamics, teaching methods, and humanistic psychology. These refinements have made them more easily applicable with larger numbers of men and women.

Twelve years ago Lowell Martin joined the organization as a counselor, contributing to effective client service in San Francisco and New York before going to Boston as Regional Executive. Now President and Chief Executive Officer of Bernard Haldane Associates, Inc., he is responsible for techniques that assure maintenance of its standards, for continuing public services offered by BHA to numerous non-profit organizations such as the YWCA, University of Hartford (Conn.), public service radio and TV, as well as for the recent growth of the organization.

Life Planning Theories   B

Many prominent researchers in the fields of humanistic and behavioral science started key elements of their work in the 1940s. These include B.F. Skinner, David C. McClelland, Eric Berne, Abraham Maslow, Frederick Herzberg, Carl Rogers. It is a coincidence that Bernard Haldane's practical work and investigations started at about the same time (in 1941) because their findings seem to support so many parts of the systems developed by Haldane.

Skinner's reinforcement theory, on which programmed learning practices are based, can be seen to support the System to Identify Motivated Skills. Dr. Skinner of Harvard is the father of behavioral science. The reinforcement theory, central to it, says whatever behavior is rewarded in any way—by attention, a checkmark, money, food, good feelings etc. tends to be repeated. The SIMS way of studying achievements enables the person to identify feelings of reward which accompany certain activities; then, by identifying skills common to most of those activities, he gives reinforcement to skills that can be used again and again to produce more and greater achievements.

Neither Haldane nor McClelland were aware of each other's works, when McClelland proved that nations tend to emulate the philosophies and practices of their heroes in his basic book (*The Achieving Society,* Van Nostrand, New York, 1961). In Haldane's work the person is helped to become aware of his or her own "hero" status through self-study of personal achievements. An outcome of this is a change in the self-image, a more realistic appreciation of one's potentialities, and evolvement of an attitude that encourages more effective application of one's skills.

Abraham Maslow's research into peak experiences pointed up man's search for self-actualization. Dr. Maslow's "hierarchy of values" shows that mankind moves from a basic safety and food demand upwards in four steps to the demand for self-actualization or fulfillment. Herzberg's related work on human motivation clarified the difference in attitudes of persons when they are involved in motivating or "hygienic" activities: the motivating ones tend to be challenging and growing experiences, while the "hygienic" ones tend to be sustaining at best. Haldane's independent work has shown that the basic structure of positive peak experiences can be identified in such a way as to clarify a person's self-motivated skills, and also the direction of his growth towards self-actualization.

One of Rogers' great contributions is his concept of non-directive counseling. Dr. Rogers has led the humanistic psychology movement in the area of clarifying how each person is able to find within himself the answers to his or her own problems. His approach stimulates the person to search around within himself for those answers. Haldane's work relates with this by providing a structure for self-developed feedback that helps a person become increasingly aware of strengths that enable him to function effectively, meaningfully and enjoyably. This improved awareness enlarges his ability to expand the joyful realities in his life.

Berne gave us transactional analysis, a personality theory and therapy that enables the person to perceive himself in an "O.K.—O.K." relationship with others. It turns out that Haldane's systems give each person evidence of where and how he is "O.K.," and encourage each person to relate with the "O.K." qualities of others. These days, many leaders of transactional analysis projects are integrating SIMS into their workshops.

1976 Research Report

The 200 most recent job-finders who used the SIMS system were sent questionnaires near the end of February. A month later, the study cut-off date, more than a hundred had been returned and classified. Just a few did not answer all the questions. 96 percent of those responding said the systems helped them to know more about their skills and talents; 89 percent reported they were able to use their skills more effectively; a surprising 75 percent claimed that their effectiveness had increased 20—40 percent or more; and an unexpected 29 percent announced that jobs which hadn't previously existed were created for them—around their unique patterns of talent.

The last two items suggest the possibility that SIMS helps to release "locked-up" human capital in ways that are not yet considered when economic judgments are made. It is obvious that money was invested to create new jobs, and it seems likely that this is because the users of SIMS had a way to reveal their potential productivity.

Peek Into The Future

Some things about the future are already certain. By 1985 there will be 22,200,000 young men and women between 16 and 24 in the workforce; 9,700,000 will be women. Currently, in 1980, 15 percent of them are unemployed, but that figure is half as high again for those between 16 and 19 (over 20 percent unemployed). The situation is much worse for blacks; more than a third of those between 16 and 19 are unemployed. The Joint Economic Committee of the U.S. Congress says, "prolonged unemployment increases the incidence of crime, drug abuse and other forms of behavior that can ruin a person's chance of achieving a productive life in the future." In noting these figures you should keep in mind that figures for the unemployed do not include about a million discouraged young persons who have stopped looking for jobs.

Jobs in state and local government will grow fastest, rising from 12 million now to 15.5 million in 1985. Federal government jobs are expected to drop from 2.8 to 2.1 million in 1985. The self-employed will continue to be about 6,700,000, indicating a serious drop in the percentage of entrepreneurs since total employment is expected to rise from 96,000,000 to some 107,000,000 in 1985. Part-time jobs will be less available. All this data comes from the U.S. Department of Labor report on the U.S. Economy in 1980 and 1985.

It also says the fastest growing industries will be Air transportation, Photographic equipment and supplies, Non-ferrous metal and mining, Computers and related equipment, Electronic components, Coal mining, Telephone and telegraph apparatus, Business services, Electric utilities, Hospitals. And the slowest growing ones will be Crude petroleum, water transportation, Ship/boat building and repair, Tobacco manufacturing, Local transit/bus, Motion pictures, Railroad transportation; Leather and its products, Petroleum products, Iron ore mining.

These official figures are particularly interesting because of the way they push people to think. Instead of helping persons to understand what they can do best and are motivated to do, the figures tend to push people towards training for the greatest growth industries and away from training in the slowest-growth ones. The figures also tend to limit experimentation in the slow-growth areas and in new areas.

Jobs are changing faster than ever, although job titles are not changing as fast. The fourth edition of the Dictionary of Occupational Titles, published about each ten years, appeared late in 1977. It will have over 5,200 title changes among the more than 20,000 jobs listed. Of these about 2,000 will be brand new, and some 3,000 will be dropped. This edition does *not* include sea mining occupations, astronauts and aquanauts; they are either too new to be considered as "established" jobs or there is no demand for them, one of your authors was told.

The statistics should not be allowed to confuse or steer a person away from the job freedom and fulfillment he or she wants. You can beat and change the statistics, if enough of you use the systems given in this book. Our 1976 Research Report reveals that when you know and offer your motivated skills they are seen as human capital, and this stimulates the investment of money into the creation of job opportunities. That summary report shows employers created jobs for 29 percent of the professional and management men and women who offered their motivated skills; the figure will be lower for first job seekers, but it should be over ten percent—which could influence a substantial rise in job opportunities if SIMS is widely used by young men and women.

And this permits a final prediction: Federal funds will soon be made available to high schools and colleges so that students may be able to learn—in credit courses—how to know their motivated skills and how to find jobs for themselves.

Book and Information Sources   C

There are too few books available which enable a person to appreciate his or her own strengths, what we call Motivated Skills. There also are few books which give comprehensive information about jobs and careers—single volumes that offer opportunity to explore many kinds of activities, or can refer you to sources for detailed information. The best, we believe, are in the following compilation—along with other community resources you could find useful.

1. Your most complete and available information source is the *Occupational Outlook Handbook.* published every 2 years by the U.S. Department of Labor. You can see it in libraries, in school and college placement and guidance offices. You can buy it for about $12.00 from the Government Printing Office, Washington, D.C. 20402. It gives facts on the kinds of jobs occupied by the great majority of some 95,000,000 employees in over 800 kinds of work that are detailed. Included are information on high school and post-high school courses which help prepare for different occupations; good generalized information on geographical location of jobs; which jobs are becoming more available and which less; what you can expect to earn; industries in which jobs exist; working conditions; and some sources for more information.

All information is presented from the employer's viewpoint, which really is the most reliable source of traditional facts. It points out that its job descriptions are composite ones—taken and combined from many different descriptions and employing organizations; also that cash pay rates given do not include "fringe benefits" like pensions, vacations, hospital care, etc. which can add 20% and more on a tax-free basis. Every Job Cooperative should have a copy.

2. *Resources: Recommendations for Adult Career Resources Supplement*, summarizes descriptions of available written and audio-visual career materials associated with a very wide variety of occupations. It is published by the B'nai B'rith Career and Counseling Services, 1640 Rhode Island Ave. NW, Washington, D.C. 20036. This organization also provides useful information, career charts, books and personal career guidance and placement help through its more than 21 offices in major cities across the U.S.A. Its services are available to persons of all faiths.

3. *Alternatives to Traditional Post-Secondary Education*, by S. Normal Feingold (immediate past president of the American Personnel and Guidance Association and National Director of B'Nai B'rith Career & Counseling Services) costs $1.00. Write for it to the above address.

4. *College Handbook* (Box 2815, Princeton, N.J. 08540), is $9.95 for the 1980 edition. It gives information on over 2,800 junior colleges and universities.

5. *The American Personnel and Guidance Association* (1607 New Hampshire Avenue N.W., Washington D.C. 20009) can provide information on numerous careers and colleges. Write and ask for what you want; they might have it or could refer you to it.

6. The 4th edition of the *Dictionary of Occupational Titles,* first change in more than ten years, appeared in 1977. It lists and describes over 20,000 different jobs, and gives them code numbers indicating the kinds of employers providing those jobs. It is a reference book available through the Government Printing Office (ibid), which may also be seen in many guidance and placement offices and all Youth Employment Offices. The jobs available in each

organization are just a little different from the descriptions in this important volume because they are a consensus of descriptions provided by many different employers. (Anyhow, you frequently can get the content of your job changed when you negotiate for the use of your motivated skills.)

7. *Your local librarian* knows where you can find magazines, lists of employers, other resources associated with your job information search.

8. The National Y.W.C.A., and all of its affiliated Ys, are now offering job finding help to young women throughout the country. Its 1975 booklet, *A Job At The End*, includes much input from Bernard Haldane, who also was among its editors.

9. *Youth Employment Counselors* are attached to every Employment Security Office in each city. These men and women are well-trained traditionalists, but they include a good number of exceptional counselors who don't go "by the book" and work hard to help young adults solve their job finding problems. Even if you use the systems given in this book you should also make contact with them for two reasons: it is possible for them to help you get the right job, and your modern approach to job finding could stimulate some of them to get with it.

10. *Service Clubs* (including Rotary and Business & Professional Women's clubs) usually have members who are strongly concerned with helping young men and women solve job problems. They can also be helpful in giving you contacts and information. Some will be very good.

11. There is a *Chamber of Commerce* (sometimes called Board of Trade) in every city and many towns. These institutions usually publish lists of employers in their regions, giving the names of key executives as well as what the organizations do in the way of providing goods and services.

12. Two bestselling books by Bernard Haldane may be obtained from the publishers directly, or through a local

bookstore. *How To Make A Habit Of Success*, takes the reader through the self-identification process, includes guidance on how to get a job and get a raise or promotion. Also, *Career Satisfaction and Success: a guide to job freedom*—step-by-step procedures that help a professional or management person deal with career development problems, including how to change careers and relationships with supervisors. It includes two chapters for employers on personnel selection and development. (American Management Association, 135 West 50 Street, New York, N. Y. 10020; $9.95.)

13. A popular book, well written, elitist and with a sense of humor, is *What Color Is My Parachute,* by Richard N. Bolles, Ten Speed Press, Berkley, Calif., 1972. While he bases his recommendations on adaptations of Bernard Haldane's work and those of former employees and students, he says those adaptations don't work for most people.

14. Your school or college or placement counselor should have *Making Vocational Choices: a theory of careers,* by John L. Holland (Prentice Hall, N.J., 1973). his Self Directed Search is a fine statistical tool for helping a person begin to clarify his or her career goals. A brilliant, patient and persevering student will be rewarded by following through his guidelines to choosing a career; it requires a lot of work.

15. *Business ownership* is something to be seriously considered. Almost one person in twelve is an independent income earner either as a professional or as an owner. But nearly 8 out of ten who start new ventures fail in the first two years. Many minority persons and women who might really have succeeded have often been frightened by these statistics. Because you may be thinking in limited terms about business ventures consider this: self-employed per-

165

sons include writers, shoe-shiners, musicians, seamstresses, dressmakers, cooks, odd-jobs persons who hire themselves out by the hour or day, musicians, lawyers and doctors, as well as those who have small stores, service stations, laundries and larger or smaller businesses. It takes a special kind of person to own or be a good partner in a business—and be successful at it. Advice on this can be had, free, through the *Small Business Administration* (S.B.A.) in your city or a nearby one; and you can see for yourself—through the pattern of your motivated skills—if you are likely to be successful as an entrepreneur or an enterprising businessperson. The most current books on ownership can be found through the S.B.A. or your local librarian.

In these sources of information we are not trying to give you complete information because, as we have demonstrated, we have confidence that you can find out what you need for yourself, or through your Job Cooperative. In addition we feel we have pointed out dependable sources for obtaining more information about whatever you want to know in regard to your future job or career.

Biographies of Authors   D

Bernard Haldane

BERNARD HALDANE's creativity in the world of work has earned commendation since 1946. He has been concerned with developing systems that enable individuals to find employment and job satisfaction for more than forty years. His 1980 contributions include culture-bridging for S.E. Asian refugees, the training of high school teachers to use his systems, teaching humanities Ph.D.s at the University of Washington, and training leaders of free Job Power Workshops for minority youth, women and others who need jobs but don't know how to get them.

His first public commendations came from The White House and the U.S. Department of Labor in 1946 for creating and leading a volunteer system that helped thousands of military persons make successful transitions into civilian work. (He was Associate Editor of the N.Y. Journal of Commerce at that time.) Then the Harvard Business School, in 1948, invited him to help design the placement program used by its graduates since then. Presidents Eisenhower, Kennedy and Johnson commended his work. Leading corporations, government agencies and universities—including EXXON, Corn Products, Union Carbide, the National Association of Manufacturers, and Columbia University—are using his systems for career planning and placement, personnel assessment, recruitment, upward mobility, outplacement, team building and other human resource development areas.

Dr. Haldane introduced modern career planning systems to the American Management Associations in 1958. Four years earlier he researched applications of his work with junior and senior high school students—first with the Bronx High School of Science, then with New Jersey's public schools while he was on the faculty at Fairleigh-Dickinson University. In 1964, when Haldane job-finding systems were tested against two control groups, three times as many in the Haldane groups of high school dropouts found jobs in less than half the time required by the control groups, according to a U.S. Department of Labor Report.

He founded Bernard Haldane Associates, Inc. in 1947 (president-emeritus since 1974), and now hundreds of professional counselors apply his systems in its 37 major-city offices. A study of its alumni revealed that 95% who complete the SIMS process learned new things about themselves, 75% reported they felt at least twenty-percent more productive, and 28% said new jobs were created by employers around their skills and talents. A more recent report on 5,000 of its "alumni" revealed that almost half changed careers without any need for retraining—and with an average salary increase of 39%

His books include: (1958) *Career Planning & Development;* (1960) *How To Make A Habit Of Success* — summarized worldwide in Reader's Digest, 1961, 62; (1964) *Young Adult Career Planning;* (1974) *Career Satisfaction & Success: a guide to job freedom;* (1976) *Job Power Now!* — revised in this new edition. Numerous articles and reports on his work have appeared in the Congressional Record, Argosy, Mademoiselle, Newsweek, Businessweek, Harvard Business Review, Personnel, and widely in general publications and newspapers.

Born May 1911 in England, he earned the First Certificate of the Royal College of Surgeons before reaching the United States (U.S. Citizen, 1937). After this was evaluated as a B.S., he studied psychological testing and labor relations at Columbia and New York universities, continued studying in group dynamics and humanistic areas, and earned M.A. and Ph.D. degrees in Management and Human Behavior.

He is married to the former Jean M. Kind, who's biography follows.

Jean M. Haldane

JEAN M. HALDANE, teacher, trainer and organization development consultant, has helped young women to be self-confident and fulfilled persons for more than 20 years. She is also the author of manuals, books and articles on how men, women and young people can — regardless of their religious orientation — identify patterns of faith and ministry in their lives. These include writings (with her husband) on how persons can come to know their "gifts for ministry," their best skills, talents, strengths.

Know nationally for her work on "ministry of the laity," she has worked with Dr. Haldane on clergy career development for more than twelve years, and helped him design the nationally-used process which enables them to make successful transitions into private industry careers.

She has served as co-leader with Bernard Haldane at Job Power, Career Development, Upward Mobility, Team Building, Career Assessment and other seminars and workshops for young people, women, clergy, professional persons and executives.

Born in England, National Executive of an Episcopal Church organization, and consultant to Bishops of the dioceses of Washington and Olympia, as well as to the National Church, she is a Fellow of the College of Preachers, Fellow of the Seminary of the Southwest, and has her M.A. in the Sociology of Religion (Goddard), after graduating from St. Christopher's College (seminary) in London, England. She lives with her husband in Seattle.

Lowell B. Martin

LOWELL B. MARTIN heads an international organization of career planning and management professionals; they counsel more than 10,000 management, professional, and technical men and women each year on all kinds of job problems. His work has been given prominent attention in the Congressional Record, many newspapers, professional publications and magazines, and has received nationwide T.V. coverage. Prior to becoming President of Bernard Haldane Associates, Mr. Martin organized and headed a firm offering career counseling to students of the University of California in Berkeley; directed his own nationwide training, sales, and distribution company; worked with the Bank of America and with Moore Business Forms on personnel and management development, and served the Haldane organization as a counselor and regional office manager. The management systems he originated and promoted are responsible for expansion of the Haldane organization into 40 cities throughout the United States, Canada and England. Born in Spokane, Washington, he graduated from the University of Idaho and did graduate work at the University of California in Berkeley.